Houston P ● ʼub
Survey, Analysis, and Research

General Academic, Inc.

Second Edition
Fall 2012

By Stephen Hayes and Shelby Joe
with support from Meghan Leach

This edition published September 12, 2012.

 General Academic, Inc.

2339 University Blvd., Suite C, Houston, Texas 77005
(800) 750 2060
www.GeneralAcademic.com
www.HoustonSchoolsSurvey.com

ISBN# 978-1-105-87318-8

Contents

General Academic, Inc.

Index of Profiled Schools

Indicates a public school

Dear Parent,

For nearly ten years, General Academic has helped Houston students reach and extend their potential through private tutoring, standardized test preparation, homework help, and consulting. Increasingly, our clients ask us for advice about middle and high schools such as questions about curriculum, special needs, accommodations, and admissions procedures. Finding no extant, comprehensive, and neutral document to leverage, we decided to undertake this study beginning in 2011. For this second edition, we have significantly expanded our analysis and research to include private middle schools and select, application-based public high schools and middle schools. Elementary-only schools remain a task for a future edition.

Our vision for this book is to provide the basic building blocks for you to jump-start your journey in researching, applying to, and selecting a private or select public school for your child. This document is not meant to replace the arguably more important steps of in-person school visits, interviews, and soul searching, but it is meant to significantly reduce the initial tedium that you would have otherwise suffered if you had started from scratch. Also, this document should enable you to quickly compare schools across a number of different criteria.

Before you dive into the convoluted school search, start by reading this document. Being the young, recent college graduates that we are—the data monkeys, writers, and analyzers of these 60,000+ words—we knew little about the stress and trials that you are about to go through or are currently going through. Therefore, we worked diligently to learn everything that we could, to answer the numerous questions that we had, and to anticipate your own. We are confident that our research will provide you with a 75% picture of what you will need to know about your middle school and high school options, comparable features, and admissions processes.

For the other, possibly more heavily weighted 25%, you will need to use some introspection, trust your instinct, and follow your eyes and ears. It is admittedly easier for us—not yet with children of our own—to advise that you take a step back and think about this whole process objectively. Nevertheless, we say it.

Please genuinely think about and consider the environment in which your child will honestly succeed. Try not to immediately assume that your oblong child will fit into square brand school. Talk to your friends, family, and school administrators about their views and experiences and trust your instinct. Finally, go see the school for yourself. Sign your child up for a shadow/buddy day so that he or she can experience a school with a currently enrolled student or administrator guide. Openly listen to what your child has to say about that experience.

All of the schools profiled here boast of the prestigious high schools and colleges where their graduates go. Like college, private secondary school is more about fit and what your child makes of it versus name recognition. With enough tenacity, spirit, and support, we are confident that your child will stand out and succeed regardless of the school that he or she attends.

Good Luck!

Shelby A. Joe
President
General Academic, Inc.

This is one of those intentionally left blank pages. If it weren't blank, the next page would be on the wrong side of a double-sided page!

The Next 2 Decades

For first time parents, the unknowns about academic deadlines can be stress inducing. In this section, we aim to alleviate some of that stress by alerting you to potential milestones for which you may want to prepare.

Many parents anxiously ask us when to start preparing their children for certain impending, academic milestones—often months or even years before they need to start preparing. We find that the best way to relieve that anxiety is by laying out a clear timeline of events, which may or may not apply to your child.

Grade	If...	Then...
Pre-Kindergarten	You want your child to attend a private school, many schools will start accepting children as young as two years old. Gaining admission into a PreK – 12 school will mean that you only have to go through this process once!	Start researching schools and preparing applications before your child's second birthday. Applications are usually due in the January of the calendar year that your child will matriculate. Expect to submit your child to a battery of IQ tests such as the WPPSI.
Kindergarten	Kindergarten is another "prime entry point" for many private schools.	Prepare your application for submission by January of the planned matriculation year.
6	Sixth grade is a prime entry point for most public and private middle schools.	Prepare your application for submission by January of the planned matriculation year. Prepare your child for the ISEE standardized test.
7	You want your gifted and talented child to participate in Duke University's TIP summer programs, seventh grade is the first year that many students will take the SAT and/ or ACT to qualify for this opportunity.	Register for the Duke Talent Identification Program national talent search and sign-up to take the SAT or ACT. Students scoring in the top 10% by grade level generally qualify for the program's highest recognition.
9	Ninth grade is the only prime entry point for both private and public high schools. Admission after 9th grade is very difficult because open spaces are usually only available due to attrition.	For private schools, register for ISEE and/or HSPT admissions tests. Applications are generally due by early January of the matriculation year for both private and public schools.

10	Students may take the Practice SAT (PSAT) and the Practice ACT (PLAN) for the first time. This exam is actually a "practice, practice" exam since the PSAT doesn't actually count for scholarship awards and recognition until 11th grade.	Relax, if your school offers these exams, your child will be automatically enrolled and given the test during a normal school day. 9th and 10th grades are the calm years before the storm of college applications!
11	1. PSAT for National Merit 2. SAT and/or ACT 3. Step Up Community Service (some private schools begin community service requirements in 9th grade)	At the start of 11th grade, do some serious reading or consult a college counselor about getting ready for college.
12	College Applications	Start preparing applications the summer before senior year, send out before Christmas, and then enjoy the second semester!
13	Gap Year. While not admittedly that popular in the United States, some students may want to take a year off between high school and college. Popular activities include living/working/volunteering abroad.	Try to research and apply to Gap Year programs before January of your matriculation year. You can also complete college applications senior year as usual and, if accepted, likely defer matriculation for a year.

This is one of those intentionally left blank pages. If it weren't blank, the next page would be on the wrong side of a double-sided page!

Considerations for Choosing a School

Systematically evaluating and comparing the many school options in Houston is a daunting task, especially when each child and family emphasizes different criteria. In this section, we introduce the categories that we used in researching the schools profiled here. Please remember that the most important criteria—your child's fit and happiness— cannot be quantified in the pages that follow. Categories that we do cover include religious affiliation, location and facilities, admissions, academic tracks and curriculum, special needs, arts, technology, extracurricular activities, and athletics.

Public Versus Private

Like so many divisive issues in American society, the decision between selecting a public versus private school usually comes down to a debate between parties who have no intention of changing their minds. However, partisans of either side of the debate should rejoice in that Houston offers great options whichever route they decide to choose. Although this discussion is beyond the scope of this book, we do provide some numerical data in the profile and summary analysis section.

Religious Affiliation

Parents looking into private schools will find that the overwhelming majority of them in Houston, nearly 70% of the schools we profiled in this book, are religious affiliated schools and within this group nearly 30% are Catholic affiliated: Baptist (2), Catholic (8), Episcopal (4), Jewish (2), Presbyterian (1). This affiliation can have broad implications for students, including compulsory daily worship, required religion classes, and differing methodologies and perspectives presented in the curriculum. Parents of children not ascribing to the school's stated faith should think carefully about how comfortable their children will be in a religious setting. However, parents should also know that most of the schools here are tolerant of other faiths and, in fact, openly embrace them. When weighing the different options, parents will be well served by asking about the school's policy on diversity and inclusion.

Location and Facilities

In general, the schools profiled here, public and private, are all in relatively safe neighborhoods; HISD schools in particular are secured further by their own police force. However, because Houston traffic tends to be trying at best, parents should consider the distance from the school to their home and accessibility to major roads. As for facilities, some schools definitely stand out above other schools in terms of newness, expansiveness, and quality of facilities. However, it is also usually the case that schools with older or more limited facilities will have ambitious plans to expand during a time frame that would still benefit a newly admitted child. Finally, athletic facilities tend to have the most variability, with schools further from Houston's city center benefitting from more space.

Admissions

The admissions process is generally straightforward and well defined by schools. Parents can anticipate the following:

1. **Application**
    a. Family background
    b. Student's academic records (if applicable)
    c. Teacher recommendations
    d. Student short answer questions
2. **Standardized Testing**
    a. ISEE or HSPT (Private and Catholic schools only)
    b. OLSAT or similar IQ test
3. **School Visits**
    a. Attending an open house

   b. Shadowing a currently enrolled student or faculty member
   c. Interviewing with the admissions department (Private Schools Only)

While the process is well defined, it's the deliberations behind closed doors that are not. Unlike major colleges and universities, most secondary schools do not publish statistics or concrete advice about what kind of student they seek.

Finally, nearly all of the schools profiled here openly acknowledge giving preferential admissions treatment to certain applicants. For most schools private and public magnet, preferential treatment works in two ways. Some schools will examine and decide on applications from preferred applicants before reviewing general applicants, meaning that there are fewer spaces available. Other schools state that they use preferential treatment only as a tie-breaking tool for when two students are identical.

For religious schools, members of the specific church (not denomination) associated with the school usually receive priority enrollment decisions. For nearly all schools, siblings of currently enrolled students, children of alumni parents, and children of faculty members generally receive preferential treatment. For some schools, the number of applicants receiving preferential treatment can easily exceed 50% of the applicant pool, making it difficulty for families not already in the school's "community."

Academic Tracks and Curriculum

Since not all children are the same, parents should look for schools with multiple academic tracks and broad curriculums to fit their specific child's need. Fortunately, many of the schools profiled here have at least three academic tracks: on-track, honors, and Advanced Placement / International Baccalaureate. The areas where schools tend to differ is:

1. How many honors and AP classes they offer
2. When students are eligible to take more advanced classes (i.e. 10th or 11th grade)
3. The maximum number of advanced classes the school allows a student to take

Graduation requirements vary from school to school but generally require a similar number of credit hours (1 hour equals one year of study): English (4), Math (3), History (3), Language (2), Art (2) Electives (2), Technology (1). Where schools tend to differ is on the math, history, language, and elective components. Most schools only require three years of math study, while a small fraction requires four. Similarly, two years of study in the same language is the general foreign language requirement, but some schools require three and even four years of study.

When requirements are lower in a core subject area like math or foreign language, the amount of time for electives rises. Most schools generally characterize art, technology, many social science classes, and very advanced core subject classes as electives.

We discuss Public School graduation requirements in-depth in the next section.

Special Needs

When evaluating schools for a child with special needs, parents should ask about the school's accommodation and modification policies. By Federal law, most schools are required to accommodate for diagnosed learning differences (extended test timing, typing assignments versus writing, etc.), but they are not required to be happy about it. The law does not require schools to modify curriculums (i.e. teach at a different pace versus an on-track curriculum). All private schools will accommodate minor to mild learning differences within their ability; however unlike public schools, they will generally not modify curriculums to better suit an individual student's needs.

Students with learning differences will find extreme differences in the level of accommodations and/ or modifications that they will receive from school to school. When a student with a diagnosed learning disability enrolls at a public school, that school is legally obligated to provide a wide range of services that we discuss further in the "Additional Considerations for Public Schools" section of this book. Conversely, main-stream private schools must only provide a basic level of accommodation that often times does not meet the needs of students with moderate to severe learning differences. For these types of students wishing to attend a private school, there are at least two private schools profiled in this book that specifically cater to students with special needs such as ADHD, dyslexia, dysgraphia, and memory retention learning differences. The other schools, even when not specifically cited, will accommodate students with diagnosed learning differences.

Furthermore, a handful of private schools employ counselors to help students who may not have diagnosed learning disabilities but could still benefit from additional learning assistance beyond that offered in on-track curriculum classes.

Arts

The breadth and depth of a school's arts curriculum is almost directly proportional to its enrollment size. The smaller schools profiled here will offer basic visual arts and music classes. However, some of the larger schools—more than 100 students per grade—have much larger offerings that would rival some small colleges. They might offer upwards of 50 classes ranging from studio art to guitar to acting and photography. The schools with the larger art departments also usually have more flexibility in graduation requirements, thereby allowing students to take advantage of their non-core curriculum offerings.

Technology

Texas requires all accredited schools teach the equivalent of a one-year technology curriculum in high school. Some of the schools profiled here satisfy that requirement through their laptop programs. These laptop programs require that each student purchase or lease a designated laptop from the school for use in class.

Nearly all schools offer at least two or three basic computer classes; some schools offer more advanced classes such as web design and AP Computer Science. Additionally, all of the schools have computer labs available for student use, and generally find some way to integrate daily technology use into the curriculum.

Extracurricular Activities

Extracurricular activities can help provide students with balance and learning opportunities outside of the core curriculum. Examples of competitive activities include speech and debate, mock trial, Model UN, quiz bowl, math club, and student government. Artistic activities include dance, bagpipes, and calligraphy.

Extracurricular activities include almost anything under the sun at most schools as long as students can find a faculty member to sponsor the activity through a club. Parents should know that the quality of most student run clubs vary widely from year to gear depending on the student leadership and membership.

Athletics

No school here requires students to participate in competitive sports, but they do all have general physical fitness requirements. Many of the schools include athletics as one of their core values. Most of the schools profiled here field interscholastic men's and women's teams in a variety of sports including: baseball, basketball, cross-country, field hockey, football, golf, lacrosse, soccer, swimming, softball, tennis, track, volleyball, and wrestling. Parents should inquire as to how many teams a school fields in each sport. For example, schools that have dedicated teams for freshman or intramural teams will allow more students to participate in the sport even if not competitively.

Athletic facilities at schools vary widely. Some schools have brand new, state of the art facilities that would put moderate size colleges to shame with their new Olympic size swimming pools, four gyms, and three game fields. However, schools in more urban locations do not usually enjoy the same luxury of space as the more suburban schools. Finally, schools with older or less accommodating often are actively fundraising to build or expand their offerings.

The high schools profiled here generally compete in the following three leagues:

1. Texas Association of Private and Parochial Schools (TAPPS)
2. Southwest Preparatory Conference (SPC)
3. University Interscholastic League (UIL)

Cost

Education is expensive. Whether parents pay through taxes or tuition, the cost is real and may very well be an important factor for families. Excluding the sunk cost of property taxes and/or a rent payment (which factors in taxes) public schools require no new cash outlay. Conversely, private schools in Houston average nearly $18,000 a year. Private school tuition is not generally tax deductible.

This is one of those intentionally left blank pages. If it weren't blank, the next page would be on the wrong side of a double-sided page!

Select Public Schools

Additional Considerations and Information for Application-Based Magnet and Vanguard Schools

Houston has some great public schools with application-based programs in a wide variety of fields. In this section, we talk about some public school specific considerations and background information.

Application and Zoned Schools

This book focuses on schools falling mostly within Houston Independent School District (HISD); the one exception is Westchester Academy, which lies within Spring Branch ISD. As the largest school district in Texas and seventh largest in the United States, HISD covers all the public schools within the 610 loop and a significant portion outside the inner loop as well. In some areas, HISD extends all the way to Beltway 8. Currently, Terry Grier is the superintendent of HISD. SBISD is located northwest of Houston, just outside the 610 loop. Currently, Duncan Klussmann is the superintendent of SBISD. Both HISD and SBISD are independent, which means that they are separate from the municipal government.

With very little exception, public schools only accept students residing within the boundaries of the school's district, which means the student's place of residence must be within the district's boundaries. In fact, a public school will usually only accept students living within the zoned area of that school. All comprehensive public schools have a designated area from which they pull students. If the student lives within that area, the student will attend that school. However, for this book, we have chosen only schools that accept students from anywhere within the school's district. If you want your child to be zoned for a particular school, buy a house in that school's zone. Your realtor should know to what schools each house is zoned.

Texas Public School Graduation Requirements

In Texas public high schools, each semester is half a credit. In some cases, high schools will accept some middle school credits, usually Algebra I and the first year of a foreign language. Check with your child's middle school to find out exactly which credits will transfer to high school. Texas offers two different types of diplomas: Recommended and Distinguished. Students must complete 26 credits to earn a Recommended Diploma (for 9th grade students entering school in 2012-2013 academic year).

English (4)	Social Studies (4)
Math (4)	Science (4)
Foreign Language (2)	Physical Education (1)
Speech (1/2)	Fine Art (1)
Electives (5 and 1/2)	

At the expense of an elective, students must take one more year of a foreign language to earn a Distinguished Diploma:

All public school courses are based on the Texas Essential Knowledge and Skills (TEKS) set by the Texas Education Agency (TEA). The TEKS are a list of objectives or concepts that the students will learn in each course. They can be found on TEA's website (www.tea.state.tx.us).

Admissions

Magnet schools are those that accept students from anywhere in the district regardless of geographic zoning boundaries. In order to gain "magnet" recognition, the school must offer a special program as its magnet. For example, a school might offer a program for only Gifted/Talented (G/T) students, or it might offer a program in a specific subject area, such as foreign languages or fine arts. Usually these schools receive more applications than they can accommodate, so they will have a lottery.

Every student who qualifies will have his or her name put into a pile, and the school will randomly select names from the pile. The selected students then receive offers of admission.

A number of the schools profiled here are simultaneously "comprehensive" and "magnet." Lanier Middle School, Pershing Middle School, Bellaire High School, and Lamar High School in HISD have magnet programs that pull from all over the district, but they are also comprehensive schools, meaning they also have zoned areas. Students residing in those zoned areas can attend those schools without applying to the magnet programs. However, if the student still wants to participate in the magnet program, for some schools, the student must still apply (see the individual school profiles for more details). The general application process is:

- Applications are usually due the first week of January, but to be safe, fill out the application early. Vanguard programs have a different application from the other magnet programs. Also, most schools have individual supplementary materials, check the individual school profiles and with the schools themselves to make sure you have all the supplementary materials.
- If your child needs testing, an audition, or an interview, the school will not schedule those appointments until after the application and supplementary materials have been submitted.
- If the school offers a day to shadow another student, take the opportunity.
- Admissions decisions will go out in March, and in most cases, the school will not give you any information before then about the admissions decision.

Gifted / Talented and Vanguard Programs

Children who function at an above average level can be tested for the Gifted/Talented (G/T) designation. Most G/T children love to learn, learn faster than their peers, and exhibit creativity or insight in their thoughts and actions.

In order for a student to receive the title of Gifted/Talented (G/T), a parent, a teacher, or the student must nominate the student for testing. As well as the student's G/T test results, the G/T Admissions Committee at the student's school will also take into account the student's grades, scores on other standardized tests, and teacher recommendations. All the student's data will go into the G/T Matrix, which is a document that assigns point values to the various pieces of data. If the total points add up to G/T qualification, the student then receives the G/T title. Parents and teachers may appeal a non-qualifying decision if they have test scores or grades to add to the student's G/T Matrix. Note that students who qualify as G/T in elementary must re-test in 5th grade to qualify for G/T status in middle and high school.

Vanguard programs work to meet the needs of G/T students; it is a type of magnet program. Vanguard Neighborhood programs operate on non-G/T campuses to meet the needs of G/T students. All teachers of G/T students will have G/T training in order to meet G/T students' needs at all schools. Vanguard Magnet programs are campus-wide programs, so the whole school is specifically for G/T students.

Special Needs

All public schools must accommodate students with special needs; however, this does not mean that magnet schools or programs have to accept students with special needs. Only if the student meets the admissions requirements of the magnet school/program, and only if the school accepts the student, does the magnet school/program have to accommodate the student.

Students may receive accommodations through the special education department or through 504. Special Education includes: learning disabilities, autism, Asperger's, physical disabilities, ADD/ADHD, and mental disabilities. 504 includes students traditionally associated with special needs as well as broadens the definition to include students with emotional issues, such as a child with anger management issues.

If you believe or know that you have a child with special needs, contact the school's special education department to find out what you need to do for your child to receive accommodations. While every public is school is obligated to accommodate students with special needs, some will only provide the minimum while others will go above and beyond what the law mandates. No child may be evaluated for accommodations without a parent's consent.

Once the process has started, a committee will determine if the student needs accommodations. The committee will consist of: a district representative, an administrator (counselor, assistant principal, or dean), the special education teacher, the student's teacher, the student's parent, and the student. If the committee agrees the student qualifies for accommodations, the committee will then determine what accommodations the student receives. These accommodations will be specific to that child's needs.

If the student meets the admissions requirements for the HISD school, then the student with special needs will be accommodated. If the parents already have documentation about the student's special needs, the school will need a copy of that documentation. After receiving the documentation, the school will set up an annual "admission, review, dismiss" (ARD) meeting that the parents, the student, an administrator, a core subject teacher, a special education teacher or 504 representative, and an HISD advocate will attend to discuss the specific modifications necessary for the student and to create an individualized education plan (IEP) for the student. Every teacher will receive a copy of the modifications for the student after the ARD meeting has determined them.

If the parents want to request modifications for their child, then the special education teacher will give paperwork to the student's teachers to document the student's behavior and any modifications the teacher uses for the student. After 6 weeks of documentation, the teachers will turn in the paperwork, and the special education teacher or 504 representative will call a meeting similar to an ARD meeting. If the meeting determines that the student needs modifications, the school will document the student's special needs and follow the same procedures as above.

STARR (Standardized Testing)

According to No Child Left Behind, public schools have to show growth in English Language Arts and Mathematics. In order to accomplish this task, Texas public schools utilize standardized testing. Before the 2011-2012 academic year, Texas used the Texas Assessment of Knowledge and Skills (TAKS). The TAKS test had grade specific tests, so everyone in the same grade took the same tests: English Language Arts (ELA), Social Studies, Mathematics, and Science. Passing all four tests at the exit level (11th grade) was a requirement for graduation.

Texas adopted the "State of Texas Assessment of Academic Readiness" (STAAR) test beginning in the 2011-2012 academic year. Grade specific tests will remain for grades 3 through 8. However, for high school, STAAR tests will be subject specific. High school students will take end of course exams in: Algebra I, Geometry, Algebra II, Biology, Chemistry, Physics, English I, English II, English III, World Geography, World History, and U.S. History. Currently, all three high school English tests and the elementary and middle school writing tests are given in the middle of March. All other tests are given at the end of April.

TEA is still debating how to grade the STAAR tests, and they probably will not decide until they have the test results from the next few years. (This is the first year of STAAR tests for grades 3-9. The classes of 2013 and 2014 are the last classes to take TAKS.) While passing STAAR tests will be a graduation requirement, TEA has not decided exactly which tests and how many the student has to pass in order to graduate high school.

Accountability Ratings

Adequate Yearly Progress (AYP) is a national accountability rating for public schools. According to the Federal "No Child Left Behind Act," public schools must show progress in Reading/Language Arts and Mathematics, which in Texas is now determined by STAAR results. High schools are also judged on their graduation rates (number of students who graduate in 4-5 years) while middle and elementary schools are judged on their attendance rates. Failing to meet AYP for two years in a row has three consequences: the state restructures the school; parents receive options for their children to attend other schools, and students may obtain free tutoring provided by a third party organization.

The Texas Education Agency (TEA) bases its Accountability Rating mostly on the Texas standardized test. The current data comes from TAKS, but Texas has moved away from TAKS to STAAR, so future data will be based on STAAR results. A tiny percentage of the rating includes SAT/ACT scores, AP scores, and graduation rate. Every school's data is available on the TEA website: www.tea.state.tx.us.

How to Understand Public Schools

While AYP and TEA Accountability ratings are one way to rate public schools, they are not necessarily the best way. In order to better understand a public school, look at its SAT, ACT, and AP scores as well as ask the parents who have students going to that school. Another good question to ask is: what will make your child happy? Some students thrive in a sea of people; in that case, one of the bigger schools might be the better option. Other students prefer small groups, so a magnet school might be more appropriate. If the student has a passionate interest offered at a magnet school, that particular magnet school might be a good fit.

This is one of those intentionally left blank pages. If it weren't blank, the next page would be on the wrong side of a double-sided page!

Funding Houston Public Schools

State, District, and Parents

School funding is extremely important to the efficient and successful operation of a school. In this section, we provide some background information and detail in particular how Houston ISD allocates funding to individual campuses.

Funding Overview

Good public school funding is an essential element to the quality of a school's offerings. Funding usually directly affects a number of school aspects such as the quality of facilities, student to teacher ratio, richness of curricula, extracurricular programs, and access to supplies and technology. For an individual school in Houston ISD, annual budgeting is determined at three main levels: state, local district, and school.

Local property taxes are the heart of the Texas educational system. In 2011, the tax rate for HISD for Harris County residents was 1.1567% of a home's appraised value. Next, state budgeting determines the overall bucket of money that Houston ISD will have including whether or not some of the local property taxes must be remitted to poorer districts (HISD is a net beneficiary of state redistribution). Local district budgeting determines how much money HISD decides to allocate to each of its 279 schools. Finally, individual school management decides how to use their received funds. Outside of annual budgeting, bond issues serve as the primary mechanism to fund major capital improvements such as renovating or building new school facilities. Additionally, parents exercise additional influence through the funding provided by independent "Parent/ Teacher Organizations" (PTO).

State Budgeting

The current funding process at the state level is extremely convoluted and is the rather messy result of merging together three principle mandates on school finance: per pupil need, historical revenue, and equality across districts. Prior to 2006, school districts received their allocations using a per pupil formula system that calculated how much districts received based on the type and number of students in their systems; types of students such as indigent, handicapped, and gifted and talented received more funding versus average students.

Acting on a 2002 Texas Supreme Court ruling on high, local property taxes, in 2006, the Texas Legislature adopted the "Target Revenue" system, which required local districts to lower their property taxes. However, the state assuaged districts that they would not lose money by guaranteeing that the district would receive the same or more money it had received in the '05-'06 or '06-'07 school years, whichever was greater.

Finally, since 1993, Texas has equalized funding across districts essentially redistributing wealth from property rich districts to property poor districts. For the 2012-2013 financial year, the total estimated funds available to Texas schools is $46.3 billion of which 46% comes from local property taxes, 43% from the Texas state treasury, and 11% from federal funds.

HISD Local District Allocation

At the local district level, HISD employs a "Weighted Pupil Formula" to allocate approximately 90% of an individual school's budget. The basic formula is:

+ Weighted Attendance
+ Special Population Units
= Total Refined Units
x Per Pupil Allocation
= Basic Allocation

+ Capital Allocation
+ Small School Subsidy
= Total Resource Allocation

Weighted enrollment sums up the number of students in two groups: early education through pre-kindergarten (EE-PK) and kindergarten through 12th grade (K-12) and multiplies that sum by the average daily attendance.

- Students in EE-PK are weighted half as much as K-12 students.
- Average Daily Attendance is a percentage.

"Special Population Units" receive additional per pupil funding on top of the weighted enrollment and are as follows:

- Mobility – if over 40% of a school's enrollment is physically handicapped, the school receives additional funds (percentage of students handicapped multiplied by .1)
- Free/ Reduced Lunch – A pupil denoted as a recipient of these aid programs receives .75% additional funding
- At - Risk – A pupil denoted as "at-risk" receives .75% additional funding
- Special Education – These pupils receive 15% more funding
- Gifted and Talented – These pupils receive 12% additional funding
- Career and Technology (FTE's) – Teachers designated as working in special technology or career programs garner a school 35% more funding per full time equivalent staff member
- ELL – Pupils designated as "English Language Learners" receive 10% extra

All schools receive a "capital allocation" that in the recommended 2012-2013 school year amounted to $10 per pupil. Finally, schools designated as "small schools" receive an additional subsidy to defray the higher marginal cost of running a small operation.

The remaining 10% of a school's budget is somewhat more discretionary and includes such items as school counselors, magnet program bonuses, special education staff, utilities, custodian, and facilities additions.

The recommended 2012-2013 HISD budget totals approximately $1.5 billion. Approximately 73% of the revenue for this budget comes from local property taxes, 23% from state funds, and less than half a percent from federal funding.

Individual School Funding

HISD is one of few school districts nationwide that practices decentralized budgeting and staffing. This decentralized system means that an individual school's principal has broad discretionary authority to allocate their school's funds. For example, a principal may opt to have more school counselors at the expense of larger class sizes or new computers at the expense of tutors. Ideally, this decentralized system should allow principals to better meet the need of their school's students.

Bond Initiatives and Major Capital Improvements

Over the last decade, major improvements to HSID school facilities, such as renovation and the building of new schools, have largely been funded by two bond programs totaling more than $1.6 billion. In June of 2012, HISD announced it would put a $1.9 billion bond initiative to voters. If the initiative passes, HISD would have raised more than $3.5 billion in just over a decade to renovate, rebuild, or relocate more than half of HISD's 279 schools. The most recent initiative will be funded through a 7% HSID property tax increase phased in through 2017 and is estimated to cost the average home owner $100 more per year in 2017 versus 2012.

The Budget Shortfall and Parents

With an estimated $5.4 billion Texas state budget deficit for 2012-2013, HISD will lose out on more than $47 million in state funding. This deficit in conjunction with the overall economic malaise means that the district has had to cut spending in almost all areas. However, this pain is generally being felt across all Texas schools. For example, per pupil funding at Lamar High School for 2011-2012 was approximately $4700 versus $4900 for Memorial High School (Spring Branch ISD) and $5000 for West Lake High School (Austin, Eanes ISD).

Through the non-profit corporations of a school's Parent Teacher Association/Organization, parents have been able to pick up some of the slack for their most cherished faculty members and programs. The funds raised by these non-profit organizations are not reported in HSID's annual budget and are usually utilized in cooperation with the PTO leadership and a school's management team. However, because the PTO is a separate entity from the school, parents have the ability to target funds at specific programs that they strongly support. Some examples of the influence of PTOs include:

- Carnegie Vanguard PTO – 2011 revenue of approximately $70,000 spent primarily on teacher appreciation/support, scholarships, and library support
- Lamar High School PTO – 2010 revenue of approximately $200,000 primarily spent on financing Prom, teacher appreciation, and college information
- Pin Oak Middle School PTO – 2009 revenue of approximately $95,000 spent largely on teacher appreciation and principal's discretionary funds

Parents looking to strengthen their voice on a school's budget should strongly consider joining their school's associated PTO.

Anti-Anxiety Comparison Worksheet

Understand what you're feeling through numbers.

Trying to keep track of your feelings about different schools in your head is difficult and stressful. Use our business consulting derived worksheets to help you more analytically compare different schools. These worksheets will not make up your mind for you, but they will provide some clarification for what you are feeling.

Anti – Anxiety Worksheet for Comparing Schools

This worksheet is an analytical and yet fast and easy way to compare schools across a number of factors that matter to you. By filling out this worksheet and examining its output, you will be able to better understand the sometimes seemingly indescribable feelings you have about a certain school. Note that the worksheet should not and will not make up your mind for you; it will only apply some order to the madness that is this process!

An Excel spreadsheet that automatically calculates values for you is available on our website at www.GeneralAcademic.com.

Directions

1. In the "School Name" box, select a school to analyze and write its name in.
2. In column A, identify the discrete considerations that matter to you; the ones discussed in this section are already listed. You may want to add additional factors such as friends, family, and finances.
3. In column B, apply a weighting of how important this consideration is to you personally. Keep things simple by using a scale of 1 to 3, one being "not important," three being "very important."
4. In column C, calculate the maximum possible value by multiplying the value in column B by 10.
5. In column D, record any pertinent thoughts that come to mind for each consideration. For example, when considering "Location," you might write, "a block from my house" or "up to an hour in traffic."
6. In column E, give the consideration a score from 0 to 10; zero being "unfavorable" and ten being "favorable."
7. In column F, multiply the value in column B by the value in D and record here.
8. At the bottom of the table, calculate the maximum possible value by adding up all of the values in column C.
9. Tabulate the actual score by summing up all of the values in column F.
10. Calculate the percentage score by dividing the actual score by the maximum score. Everyone has their own thresholds, but generally a score of 80% or higher means, "I love this school," while 65-80% means, "I like this school," 50-65% means, "I would be happy with this school," 30-50% means, "I'm mostly indifferent," and a score of less than 30% means, "avoid at all cost."

Sample School Worksheet					
	A	B	C	D	E	F
#	Consideration	Weight	Max	Remarks	Score	Output
1	Religion	2	20	Unaffiliated	5	10
2	Location	3	30	Very far from home, 45 min plus	1	3
3	Facilities	2	20	Brand new buildings	10	20
4	Admissions	1	10	Good chance of getting in	8	8
5	Tracks	3	30	Lack of different options	4	12
6	Curriculum	3	30	Lots of foreign languages	10	30
7	Family	2	20	Older sister already attends	10	20

Maximum Score	Actual Score	Percentage Score
160	103	64% = I'd be happy.

School Name

#	A Consideration	B Weight	C Max	D Remarks	E Score	F Output
1	Religion					
2	Location					
3	Facilities					
4	Admissions					
5	Tracks					
6	Curriculum					
7	Special Needs					
8	Arts					
9	Technology					
10	Extracurricular					
11	Athletics					
12	Cost					
13						
14						
15						
16						
17						
18						
19						
20						

Maximum Score | | **Actual Score** | | **Percentage Score** |

School Name

#	A Consideration	B Weight	C Max	D Remarks	E Score	F Output
1	Religion					
2	Location					
3	Facilities					
4	Admissions					
5	Tracks					
6	Curriculum					
7	Special Needs					
8	Arts					
9	Technology					
10	Extracurricular					
11	Athletics					
12	Cost					
13						
14						
15						
16						
17						
18						
19						
20						

Maximum Score | | **Actual Score** | | **Percentage Score** |

General Academic, Inc.

School Name						
#	**A** Consideration	**B** Weight	**C** Max	**D** Remarks	**E** Score	**F** Output
1	Religion					
2	Location					
3	Facilities					
4	Admissions					
5	Tracks					
6	Curriculum					
7	Special Needs					
8	Arts					
9	Technology					
10	Extracurricular					
11	Athletics					
12	Cost					
13						
14						
15						
16						
17						
18						
19						
20						
Maximum Score			**Actual Score**		**Percentage Score**	

School Name						
#	**A** Consideration	**B** Weight	**C** Max	**D** Remarks	**E** Score	**F** Output
1	Religion					
2	Location					
3	Facilities					
4	Admissions					
5	Tracks					
6	Curriculum					
7	Special Needs					
8	Arts					
9	Technology					
10	Extracurricular					
11	Athletics					
12	Cost					
13						
14						
15						
16						
17						
18						
19						
20						
Maximum Score			**Actual Score**		**Percentage Score**	

School Name

#	Consideration	Weight (B)	Max (C)	Remarks (D)	Score (E)	Output (F)
1	Religion					
2	Location					
3	Facilities					
4	Admissions					
5	Tracks					
6	Curriculum					
7	Special Needs					
8	Arts					
9	Technology					
10	Extracurricular					
11	Athletics					
12	Cost					
13						
14						
15						
16						
17						
18						
19						
20						

Maximum Score | **Actual Score** | **Percentage Score**

School Name

#	Consideration	Weight (B)	Max (C)	Remarks (D)	Score (E)	Output (F)
1	Religion					
2	Location					
3	Facilities					
4	Admissions					
5	Tracks					
6	Curriculum					
7	Special Needs					
8	Arts					
9	Technology					
10	Extracurricular					
11	Athletics					
12	Cost					
13						
14						
15						
16						
17						
18						
19						
20						

Maximum Score | **Actual Score** | **Percentage Score**

This is one of those intentionally left blank pages. If it weren't blank, the next page would be on the wrong side of a double-sided page!

College Credit in High School

Advanced Placement® and International Baccalaureate® Programs

Earning college credit simultaneously with high school credit is a great way for academically gifted students to demonstrate their talents and tenacity to competitive college admissions departments. Furthermore, the successful completion of these classes also allows students to bypass the mundane, entry-level lectures that their not as fortunate college freshman classmates will have to endure. Bypassing these basic classes not only allows students to explore more interesting offerings but it can also potentially save generous parents tens of thousands of dollars.

Why Take Advanced Track Courses

Academically gifted and talented students should strongly consider taking advantage of their school's most rigorous course offerings. This suggestion is based off of at least three reasons:

1. Advanced classes feed students' desire to learn.
2. Colleges favor students who challenge themselves.
3. Students can earn college credit for classes taken in high school.

Advanced classes feed a students' desire to learn more information at a deeper level. Advanced classes move faster than their counterparts. The faster pace of these classes allows teachers to cover more topics at a deeper level. For example, an on-track biology class might read about frog anatomy out of a book while an honors class has time to read the book and actually dissect the frog in a lab.

Selective colleges favor students who challenge themselves. According to the College Board, the not for profit administrator of the AP program, 85% of selective colleges and universities report that taking Advanced Placement courses improves their chances of admission. When reviewing applicants, colleges and universities examine the courses that students take in high school. Understanding the additional effort that goes into succeeding in advanced offerings, they favor students who enroll in more difficult classes. Sometimes enrolling in more difficult classes results in lower grades. However, most high schools recognize this fact and calculate grade point averages (GPA) accordingly. For example, a school grading on a 4 point scale (A=4.0, B=3.0, C=2.0) may in fact give additional points for an honors or Advanced Placement class (A=5.0). Even if a high school does not award such bonuses, colleges are more likely to appreciate an applicant earning A's and B's in advanced classes versus a student earning solid A's in on-track classes.

Students can earn college credit for classes taken in high school. Students enrolling in Advanced Placement and/or International Baccalaureate classes are studying entry-level college material. At the completion of the class, students have the option to take an independently administered examination. Successfully completing this exam can lead to earning equivalent credits in college. For example, if a student takes the AP Exam in Computer Science A and scores a 4 or 5 (out of 5), the University of Texas at Austin will award credit for having taken its CS 312 class, a three credit hour class. A student could therefore enroll at a college as a sophomore (usually 30+ credit hours) without having taken one class (or paying tens of thousands of dollars) at the college.

Introduction to the AP and IB Programs

The Advanced Placement and International Baccalaureate programs are the two most widely offered and recognized methods for obtaining college credit for demonstrated performance in high school classes. The American non-profit organization College Board administers the Advanced Placement (AP) program; the College Board is the same organization that administers the PSAT and SAT standardized tests. The Swiss non-profit foundation International Baccalaureate Organization (IBO) administers the International Baccalaureate (IB) programs. The IBO offers four main programs depending on age, but this document will focus on the Diploma program, which is for students generally aged 16-19 or American high school juniors and seniors.

The History of AP and IB Programs

The Advanced Placement Program dates back to the end of World War II when the Ford Foundation funded two committees to help bridge the gap between secondary and higher education. The first committee included prestigious prep schools Andover, Exeter, and Lawrenceville and universities Harvard, Yale, and Princeton; the committee concluded that secondary schools and colleges should work together. The second committee was tasked with figuring out how these schools and universities should work together. The product of their labor was an 11 subject pilot program in 1952, which was then handed over to the College Board for administration beginning in 1955. Today, more than one million US high school students participate in the AP program every year.

The International Baccalaureate Organization dates back to 1948 when the "Conference on International-Minded Scholars" asked the International School of Geneva (Ecolint) to create an international schools program. The initiative gained strength when the United Nations Educational, Scientific, and Cultural Organization (UNESCO) provided a $2500 grant in 1962 (and later another $10,000) to organize an international conference of teachers about the idea. In 1964, three influential men in education—Alec Peterson of Oxford University, Harlan Hanson of the College Board AP Program, and Desmond Cole of the UN International School—came together and founded the International Schools Examination Syndicate (ISES). This project gained more support when the Twentieth Century Fund commissioned a report to establish an international education curriculum and examination system for international schools. The Ford Foundation funded additional studies on international education. This research finally culminated in a reorganization of the ISES into the International Baccalaureate Council of Foundation, which ultimately saw the IB organization headquarter in Geneva, Switzerland in 1968. Today there are over 900,000 IB students across more than 140 countries.

AP Program Fundamentals

The AP program offers high-school curriculums and examinations in approximately 34 subjects ranging from Calculus and Physics to Latin, Human Geography, and Studio Art. Schools participating in the program typically do not offer all 34 subjects. The standard offering for Houston private schools is approximately 10-15 classes.

Any student taking any class (including home-school students) can pay the approximately $80 fee to take an AP examination at a registered testing site. However, most Houston schools have rules about who can take what classes and exams. For example, some schools will not allow freshmen and sophomores to take AP classes at all while other schools may require students to earn certain grades in the class before sitting for an exam.

AP examinations are standardized tests administered at approved testing sites, which may include the host school. They are usually administered in early May and are scored on a scale of 1 to 5, with the highest score being a 5. A score of 3 is passing although many selective colleges and universities require a score of 4 or 5 to earn college credit. Rice University requires scores of 4 or 5. The University of Texas at Austin accepts a range of scores (as low as 2 for German); however, higher scores allow students to place out of a wider range of classes.

Schools wishing to offer Advanced Placement® titled classes must submit their curricula to the College Board for approval. However, even if a curriculum is not approved, students may still sit for the AP exam, often times at their school even without being enrolled in certified classes.

IB Diploma Program Fundamentals

The IB Diploma Program is a comprehensive two-year program for juniors and seniors. To successfully complete the Diploma program, students must complete three core requirements and six subject courses. The subject courses are divided into Standard Level (SL) and Higher Level (SL). Generally, students take three SL classes and three HL classes, although individual school requirements or offerings may vary. Only one of the core requirements, Theory of Knowledge, is an actual class. All subject courses culminate in a final, standardized examination.

The core requirements are Extended Essay (EE), Theory of Knowledge (TOK), and Creativity, Action, Service (CAS). Extended Essay is an independent research essay. The Theory of Knowledge Class is the one class that all IB students around the world are required to take and is a kind of philosophical introduction to the practice of learning. CAS is the extra-curricular component of the IB Diploma; it mandates that students participate in activities such as community service and sports. A counterweight to pure academics, CAS is not a class but a general expectation that students will spend approximately 3-4 hours a week involving themselves in non-academic endeavors.

Students are required to take six subject courses. More than 50 course offerings are divided into six groups: 1) Language A1 (native language) 2) Second Language 3) Individuals and Societies 4) Experimental Sciences 5) Mathematics and Computer Science 6) The Arts. Students must take one class from categories 1-5 and select the sixth from any of the six categories. Although Diploma candidates are required to take three Higher Level classes, they may take more if their school and schedules allow.

Students earn points for each of the six IB classes ranging from 1-7; additionally they may also earn up to three more points for the core requirements for a maximum possible score of 42. 24 points are required to graduate with at least 12 coming from Higher Level Subjects, 9 from Standard Level, and 3 from core requirements. Scores on the exams of 4 and above are considered passing and generally make the student eligible for college credit. More selective universities generally require a score of six or above. Rice University only grants credit for scores of 6 and 7 on Higher Level exams only. The University of Texas awards credit for a range of scores but generally requires a score of 4 or above on either Standard Level or Higher Level classes.

A Note About the IB Certificate

Students attending schools that offer the IB Diploma program may usually take IB classes but not pursue the full Diploma requirements. In this way, they may pick and choose classes just as they would if they were participating in the AP program. Students pursuing this route earn an "IB Certificate" for each Standard Level or Higher Level exam that they successfully complete.

Differences Between AP and IB

Program Philosophy

The AP program follows a "pick and choose" philosophy for both schools and students. Schools can decide what classes they will offer, and students can then select from those offerings. Alternatively, students at schools without any AP classes can still prepare for and take AP exams.

The IB Diploma is a curriculum and holistic teaching philosophy. Schools offering the curriculum must be prepared to offer the full Diploma curriculum. Classes must emphasize internationalism. The core curriculum is what most differentiates the IB Diploma. However, the IB Certificate is very similar to the AP's *À la carte* methodology.

College Credit

Students seeking the most number of college credits will probably be better served with the AP curriculum. Established in the United States and older than the IB program, American universities are more likely to award credit in a wider number of courses than they would the IB program. For example, Rice University accepts only IB Upper Level exam scores and offers nearly twice the number of aggregate credits for AP exams than it does for IB exams. If a college only accepts Upper Level exams, then an IB student is probably looking at no more than 9 to 12 credit hours (3-4 exams earning 3 hours each) versus an AP student who could theoretically take all 34 of the offered exams and earn more than 90 hours of credit. However, some IB schools will allow students to take more than three Upper Level courses, thus enabling them to earn more college credits.

IB Diploma recipients attending public colleges and universities in Texas, Florida, Colorado, and California are guaranteed a minimum of 24 hours of credit because of state legislation. Because of this legislation and increasing awareness, colleges are liberalizing their attitudes toward IB credit. Additionally, while many universities overseas award credit for the AP program, IB acceptance is more wide spread.

Breadth of Offerings

The IB program offers more choices, more than 50 to AP's approximately 35. In particular, schools offering IB programs generally have much larger foreign language selections than AP only schools—even if the school does not have a Danish teacher for example, a student may still study that language through a combination of remote learning and self-study tools offered by the IB organizers. However, each school's actual offerings will vary.

Fine Choices

The AP and IB programs are both excellent ways for students to study at a deeper level, push themselves, and earn college credit. Realistically, once admitted to a school, students will unlikely have the option to choose between the two programs as the school will have already made the choice. (Exception being that anyone can take an AP exam). Regardless, Parents and students cannot go wrong with either program.

Advanced Placement® is a registered trademark of the College Board. International Baccalaureate is a registered trademark of the International Baccalaureate Organization.

This is one of those intentionally left blank pages. If it weren't blank, the next page would be on the wrong side of a double-sided page!

Houston Private & Select Public Schools

Alternative Curricula
Montessori and Homeschooling

Not every child will be successful or happy in a traditional classroom environment. For these students, alternative education curriculums such as Montessori and home schooling may be better options. Although Montessori school techniques can vary widely from school to school, this teaching method generally strives to offer a comparatively more nurturing and holistic learning environment than strictly score based curriculums. Texas provides excellent legal guidelines and latitude for parents considering homeschooling. Although homeschooling does provide the most flexible of curriculum, it's important to understand what future educational institutions will expect when deciding what children will learn.

Why Choose a Montessori or Homeschooling Curricula

Alternative forms of education offer students different opportunities from the standard American curriculum. The pace and structure of the lessons are individualized and students are more personally responsible for their own education. Alternative curriculums are afforded more flexibility than their traditional counterparts; however, it is important for these curriculums to match the requirements of accredited public and private institutions in order to maximize acceptance by colleges. When deciding on joining an authentic Montessori school or beginning a homeschool curriculum for a student, a parent should take into consideration:

1. Alternative forms of education involve a different social atmosphere from traditional private and public educations
2. The Montessori curriculum does not grade or test its students in the same manner as traditional schools, including most colleges and universities
3. Some students require very specialized help, which might not be conducive to the Montessori Method or a parent teaching his child
4. Not all Montessori programs are created equal
5. A homeschooled student in Texas is considered the same as a student who attends a non-accredited private school
6. Each student is unique; determine what education style suits your child best

A History of the Montessori Method

Dr. Maria Montessori (1870-1952), an Italian physician and educator, began developing the Montessori Method in 1897, while attending pedagogy courses at the University of Rome. She focused on the educational theory of the last two hundred years preceding her research and began to question the traditional methodologies of education. To Dr. Montessori, an individual truly learns through interacting with one's environment, especially when freely allowed to choose with what one interacts. Ten years later, Dr. Montessori opened her first educational facility called Casa dei Bambini, a childcare center in Rome. Since then, her theories have been implemented in over 22,000 Montessori schools worldwide.

The Montessori Method initially broke ground in the United States in the early 1900s with 100 schools established in 5 years, but the method immediately conflicted with the traditional American system of education. William Kilpatrick, an influential voice in education at the time, and his critical piece *The Montessori System Examined* further limited the spread of the Montessori Method in the United States. By the 1920s, the movement to spread the theories of Dr. Montessori and the established Montessori schools had virtually vanished.

However, in 1953, Dr. Nancy Rambusch attended the Tenth International Montessori Congress in Paris and met Mario Montessori, Dr. Montessori's son and confidant. Impressed with the Montessori Method, Dr. Rambusch followed Mario Montessori's advice and began implementing Dr. Montessori's theories and practices in teaching her children. Five years later, Dr. Rambusch, along with a number of families, established the Whitby School in Greenwich, Connecticut. 1960 saw the birth of the American Montessori Society and its goals mirrored those of the Association Montessori Internationale. One difference divided the two organizations for a time: the American Montessori Society requires that all teachers hold college degrees so their curriculum might be recognized by state education departments. Today, there are 1,200 schools affiliated with the AMS and Montessori Method of education.

How the Montessori Methodology Works

According to Dr. Montessori, children allowed to choose and interact freely within a prepared environment achieve the greatest possible results in human development. Dr. Montessori also observed several human tendencies that are integral to each stage of development, such as:

- Self-preservation
- Order
- Work or "purposeful activity"
- Communication
- Exactness
- Repetition
- Self-perfection
- The "mathematical mind"
- Abstraction
- Orientation to the environment
- Exploration
- Manipulation of the environment

Dr. Montessori developed her curriculum to highlight these tendencies, which includes a heavy emphasis on the student's environment. Classrooms, or "prepared environments," must be kept in order and clean, leaving the walls mostly unadorned and free of clutter. The classroom must be built in proportion to the student, thus an environment for very young children would feature low tables and cabinets that can easily be accessed by the student. The classroom will only contain supplies necessary to the development of the student and the activities will be arranged in a manner that promotes movement. Dr. Montessori suggests that classrooms utilize natural light and soft colors, citing that bright colors distract students.

Dr. Montessori also structures the Montessori Method around four "planes" of development she observed in her work. In the first plane, from birth to age six, the student is a concrete learner, utilizing sense to interact with and understand one's environment while developing intelligence and the psychological self. During this stage, the student has an "absorbent mind" which seamlessly assimilates information from the senses, culture, and language and develops ideas. In the second plane, ages 6 to 12, students have a tendency to socialize and work in groups, or "herd instinct," while their abilities to reason and imagine flourish. Dr. Montessori encompasses adolescence in the third plane, ages 12 to 18, where students are psychological unstable, concentration is difficult, and they strive for "valorization," or the drive for an external evaluation of worth and ability. The fourth and final plane, ages 18 to 24, received less attention from Dr. Montessori and she did not develop an educational format for this plane. She believed students of the Montessori Method would be well prepared to face the adult environment.

One of the main aspects of the Montessori Method is the multi-age groupings of students in the classroom. Children are not separated by grade, but are grouped together with students who are younger or older. An authentic Montessori program will group students together whose ages usually span 3 years apart. In this sense, the older students, who have recently mastered a particular lesson, are able to support the younger students in their own lessons. The older student reinforces the ideas of the mastered lesson and the younger student receives a mentor, or a big "brother" or "sister," to look up to. Dr. Montessori considered the traditional designation of grades to be arbitrary, preferring the creation of these multi-age groups, as opposed to separating students by a single age, with the goal of developing stronger communities within the classroom.

Within a Montessori curriculum, students work at their own pace and interest. Students do not receive grades, but students must demonstrate a very high percentage of accuracy in testing in order to move from one lesson to the next. Teachers do not act as lecturer but as a guide to the student, thus creating a triangle of education between the student and classroom environment. As a guide, the teacher will initially demonstrate the activities to the student, but will mostly observe the child's development. The teacher might provide the student with small nudges, but the student discovers the information independently and engages in self-correction.

Determine the Authenticity of the Montessori School

"Montessori" is within the public domain, thus any school may apply the name to its institution without adhering to any of Dr. Montessori's theories or practices. It is important, then, for parents to determine the authenticity of a school's practices if they wish for their student to be educated with the Montessori Method. Generally, authentic Montessori facilities feature:

1. Multi-age classes, where older students act as mentors to younger students
2. A complete assortment of Montessori learning materials
3. Teachers who are certified through a recognized Montessori education training program
4. Teachers who adhere to the instructional practices of the Montessori Method, acting as guides and not lecturers
5. An affiliation or accreditation with the American Montessori Society or the Association Montessori Internationale

The middle school to high school curriculum will vary from school to school, as Dr. Montessori did not fully develop an educational curriculum for this age period. If a student wishes to attend a university or college, it is important to take in consideration how closely the Montessori's high school curriculum matches state standards. However, Montessori schools tend to integrate state approved educational practices with the Montessori Method, thus making its students more accepted by state institutions.

Choosing Homeschooling

The state of Texas treats home schools the same as non-accredited private schools. To this extent, parents have great flexibility to teach or have an instructor teach their children in the manner that they see most fitting. However, parents planning to interact with accredited public and private schools will want to ensure that the home-school curriculum closely mirrors the accredited institution and that their children can pass tests to demonstrate a mastery of the material.

The state of Texas enforces very few requirements on parents wishing to home school their children. The law is very explicit in stating that state colleges must not discriminate against applicants who have been home schooled. The state really only exercises involvement when the parent needs to interact with the public school system or comply with compulsory school attendance laws:

1. Notification of disenrollment from the school
2. Personal assurance that the student is being home schooled properly
3. Verification of curriculum if wishing to re-enter public school

Texas law gives local school officials the authority to make "reasonable inquiry" as to whether children are actually being properly homeschooled. According to the open letter published by the Texas Education Agency, this inquiry should only seek written assurance that the student is being properly home schooled. School districts are not required to seek verification. Properly home schooled is defined by these three rules:

1. The student is actually receiving real instruction
2. The curriculum is based on tangible items such as books and videos
3. The curriculum includes instruction in reading, spelling, grammar, math, and good citizenship

Although the curriculum must include some basic buckets, parents may have complete control as to what information goes into those buckets and how it's taught. Additionally, parents may have other parents teach their children or pay for a tutor to come to their home.

Texas's laws pertaining to home schooling are based on the Texas Supreme Court ruling in March of 1985 in the case of Leeper v. Arlington I.S.D.

Creating the Homeschool Curriculum

Aside from requirements designated by Texas law, parents of homeschooled children may craft the curriculum in any manner they see fit. The parent may choose to instruct the student or choose another individual to act as their student's teacher. If the ultimate goal is to have the student return to an accredited public or private school, or even a college or university, then the curriculum should closely mirror the standards of Texas Essential Knowledge and Skills. There are also a number of homeschool curriculums available for use, such as Laurel Springs and Texas Tech (TTUISD).

In regards to extracurricular activities in Texas, the decision to allow home-schooled students to participate in a public school's extracurricular activities such as band, choir, and athletics is left up to locally elected school boards. However, home schooled students will not usually be allowed to participate in events sponsored by the University Interscholastic League (UIL), since that league requires that participants be full-time students enrolled in the participating school. Parents are free to register their students in non-scholastic athletic leagues and competitions of which there are a wide number and diverse set in Houston. Parents may even want to consider hiring an art or music teacher to teach their students as well.

Returning to an Accredited School Environment

The home school curriculum only comes under real scrutiny when parents wish to re-enter their student into an accredited institution at grade level. The TEA has determined that students transferring from home schools to accredited public schools be treated the same as students transferring from non-accredited private schools. The TEA only instructs that local school districts assess a student's fitness by administering "valid and reliable assessment instruments." The TEA does not regulate which instruments (evaluations) a school may or must use; this determination is left up to the local school district. It suggests only that local public school administrators place students based on a review of the curriculum, course of study, and quality of work output. The TEA does however make some recommendations for assessment:

1. Elementary students should be assessed using a nationally recognized test such as a previously released TAAS or TAKS exam applicable to the grade level the student seeks qualification in.
2. Secondary school students be assessed using the "credit by examination" (CBE) method or by a previously released TAAS or TAKS exam.

TAKS stands for Texas Assessment of Knowledge and Skills and has been Texas's state standardized test since spring of 2003. The test is designed to measure to what extent a student has succeeded in learning the curriculum as defined in the Texas Essential Knowledge and Skills (TEKS). More information can be obtained online at the TEA's website. Note, that beginning in Fall 2011, Texas now uses the State of Texas Assessments of Academic Readiness test (STAAR).

Credit by examination basically means that the local school district tests a student's subject knowledge and then makes a determination as to whether or not the student is at grade level. Texas gives wide latitude to local school officials to determine the criteria for these examinations. The Houston Independent School District (HISD) has documented procedures for CBE:

1. Exam Dates – The school district will allow students to test on 6 dates throughout the year. For grade 6-8, these dates are three days in June and three days in July. For grades 9-12 the test dates are in 3 days in November and June. Exact dates are published on HISD's Student Assessment Testing Calendar.
2. Obtaining a CBE – Parents should contact the principal or counselor of the school to which they are interested in enrolling their student. This school official will counsel the parent on appropriate procedures and require a written application.
3. Passing the CBE – Home school students are treated as "having prior instruction" in the subject material; therefore, a student must only score higher than a 70% to consider as having passed.

For private schools, the admissions procedures may vary slightly from these detailed for public schools, and parents should consult with individual private school counselors on their procedures. However, parents should expect that private schools will require that the student pass a standardized test for admission to the school and a CBE for entry into a certain grade level.

Determining Instructor/s for your Homeschool Curriculum

Historically, parents have served as the primary educator in home schooling environments. However, not all parents have the academic skills or time to serve as their student's full time instructors. In this case, parents may want to seek outside instructors, and may do so through different avenues.

Hiring a single in-home instructor is naturally the first course of action. The advantage with this strategy is that the student has a single point of interaction and can foster a strong relationship with his instructor if there is good chemistry between the two. There are possible obstacles to finding and hiring this instructor. Primarily, it may be difficult for parents to temporarily hire an individual for what is essentially a full time job. Additionally, there are hurdles in finding, interviewing, and legally contracting with the individual.

Managing multiple tutors is another option. The advantage to this avenue is that it's easier to find qualified individuals who are willing to commit several hours a week versus their entire day. Furthermore, it may be easier to fill certain academic skill sets depending on the difficulty of the material. The disadvantage with multiple tutors is the risk that the student doesn't build a strong relationship with his instructors. Additionally, parents may have trouble managing the various tutors and ensuring a cohesive curriculum.

Personal networks are the first source for new hires. Parents can talk to neighbors and friends who have used tutors in the past or home schooled their children; additionally, the school that the parents are withdrawing from or the target school for re-entry may also maintain a list of tutors and instructors who might be interested.

Use established, outside recruitment resources. When personal networks don't yield desirable results, parents can also use sites like Craigslist or even Careerbuilder and Monster to post a job description. Craigslist is free and, despite its sometimes less than stellar reputation, can often yield very excellent candidates. Monster and Careerbuilder are relatively expensive and often result in an excess of steps but should still be regarded as an option. Finally, if parents are looking for a specific skill-set, they would be well served to consult with local colleges and universities. These centers of higher education often maintain direction connection with undergraduates and graduates majoring in these academic areas and can easily solicit on your behalf.

Screening Applicants

Parents should pre-screen applicants based on educational background and teaching experience. Standardized test scores such as the ACT, SAT, LSAT, GMAT, and GRE are a great place to start. Ask for current or graduating GPA and an academic transcript, while paying close attention to the subject areas that you'll want the individual to teach. However, remember that great test scores do not a perfect teacher make. Also look for previous teaching and/or tutoring experience. Volunteer experience is great and many years of service can demonstrate that the individual has a passion for learning. Paid experience is possibly more valuable than volunteer experience because it is more analogous to the paid work that the applicant will be doing for you.

It is important to set up in-person interviews with an interactive component that demonstrates the individual's ability to instruct your student. Discuss the candidate's resumed, background, education, and work experience. After interacting with the candidate, ask the candidate to spend some time teaching your student one-to-one in a subject area. Follow up with the student to see if there is any potential chemistry between the student and instructor. It's best to have at least two adults present for the discussion portion of the interview. Two individuals will help ensure that all of the right questions are asked and provides more than one perspective. Parents should repeat this interview process at least twice for successful candidates.

Interviewing and Hiring

For successful candidates, after conducting at least two interviews, parents should ask for social security numbers and previous addresses to conduct a background check. Parents must inform the candidate they are performing a background check and let the candidate notify their references that they will be contacted soon. Additionally, parents should secure the candidate's written consent to conduct the check, especially if parents plan on checking the candidate's credit. Here are some steps to validate a candidate:

1. Education – Contact schools directly or go through a clearing house
2. Experience – Check with references
3. Crime – Use a third party verifier to search state and federal records
4. Sex Abuse – Search state sex offender databases
5. Credit – Use a third party verifier

It would be wise for parents to have a list of at least two individuals qualified for hiring. Do not reject anyone on this "acceptable list" until receiving a written letter of acceptance from the top pick. If an applicant is rejected, inform the applicant of the reasons why and offer to refer them to other sources for hiring.

It is important to ensure that the hiring is legal. Depending on a parent's exact requirements, one must decide whether the instructor will be an employee or a contractor. The difference is significant in how the IRS collects and expects the parent to report earnings. Consult with an attorney if there is any doubt in how to proceed in this area.

Once parents hire outside help, they must actively manage the instructor and student. The instructor will still likely need the parents' help in ensuring that the student adequately completes his/her homework (there is still plenty of homework in a home school environment). Additionally, parents will want to ensure that the instructor is adequately teaching the curriculum and that the instructor has access to the resources needed to succeed. In addition to casual conversation, parents would be well served to establish a formal performance evaluation to ensure that their instructor(s) are performing to expectations.

Introduction to the Applications Process
Lessons Learned and Timeline

In this section, we provide advice on beginning the process of applications including lessons learned from experienced parents and a recommended timeline. In general, start the process early, keep your child's happiness in mind, and talk with as many people as possible.

Parent Lessons Learned

We interviewed the parents of both private and public school students to more completely understand the applications gauntlet from those who had already been through the process. These parents were our clients at the time and represent a broad range of backgrounds. For example, we talked to a mother who was born and raised in Houston and another who had only recently been transferred to the US by her international company. We talked to the parents of children who are in the top 1% by test scores and others whose children were in special needs schools. Some parents described themselves as extremely religious while others said they preferred to have no religious affiliation at all. Despite these perceived differences and outlooks on life, they still managed to agree on many of the same things.

Here are the top five nuggets of wisdom that these parents provided us:

1. **Be objective about your child's talents and aspirations.**
   Almost all parents agreed that the "right school" was more about individual fit and environment versus perceived name recognition and curriculum. The word used most often was, "objective." Talking about not pushing parents' dreams on kids, one St. John's parent even went so far as to say, "Don't be so invested...don't let them know how much you want them to get in." A School of the Woods mother says, "It's only middle and high school, don't worry so much...if they love learning, they will carry that with them no matter the school."

2. **Consider, visit, and apply to many schools.**
   Most parents advised first-timers to visit many schools, not just a handful of the "big names" and to "ignore the noise." Make sure to give yourself options by applying to multiple schools including a "stretch" and a "safety."

3. **Talk not only with current parents but also the students.**
   Most parents are good about talking to other parents and asking admissions directors copious amounts of questions, but they often forget to talk to the students! The students are the ones who are experiencing these schools first hand, every day, for 8 hours a day. An Emery-Weiner parent says, "Ask the kids what they think about the schools...most parents are followers. They don't know what goes on behind the doors but the kids are living it every day."

4. **Rest easy in that the applications process itself is not that terribly daunting.**
   Parents seemed to agree that the actual application process, once underway, was relatively easy. They stated that the forms and deadlines were clear and that admissions officers were easy to talk to. When asked what obstacles parents faced when applying, the word that was used most often was, "none."

5. **Make your life easier by applying early and timely.**
   The simple advice here is not to procrastinate. This wisdom is especially sage when applying to schools with rolling admissions where increasingly few spots will be available as the new school year approaches. For schools with hard deadlines, being ahead of the deadline means that parents will have peace of mind earlier and time to complete anything in case the school says it was incomplete. Most parents stated that they started the applications process 3-5 months before January of the matriculation year.

Fill out our questionnaire online at www.HoustonSchoolsSurvey.com. Your responses will be kept anonymous.

Suggested Application and Admissions Timeline and Checklist

Private Schools	Public Schools

Summer Before the Year of Matriculation

• Decide on the criteria you want to use to choose a school.	
• Browse school websites; take the online tours and look at photos.	
• Request catalogs and videos from selected schools.	• Browse HISD's website for Magnet schools at houstonisd.org/magnet

Fall Before the Year of Matriculation

• Attend the Private School Preview	• Attend the Magnet Open House
• Verify and list admissions deadlines and requirements.	
• Ask teachers to complete reference forms if necessary	
• Start preparing your student for standardized admissions and/or IQ tests.	
• Start financial aid request process if needed.	• Attend Magnet Awareness Week activities at interested schools

Winter Before the Year of Matriculation

December

• Register for ISEE and/or HSPT standardized tests.	• Schedule standardized testing as required
• Complete applications.	
• Schedule school visits, interviews, and auditions as necessary.	

January

• Watch your deadlines. Beat them by a week or more if possible.	
• Take HSPT/ISEE tests.	
• Complete financial aid forms.	
• Submit school applications.	

February

- If application deadline was in January, relax!
- If applying under rolling admissions, get your application in ASAP as fewer spaces are available the longer you wait.

Spring of the Year of Matriculation

March

- Decision letters should start arriving by mid month.
- Take the appropriate action required by the letter.

April

- Let schools know your decision.
- Examine your options for schools which wait listed your child.

This is one of those intentionally left blank pages. If it weren't blank, the next page would be on the wrong side of a double-sided page!

Private School General Admissions Requirements

Admissions requirements and applications are generally well standardized from school to school. Furthermore, these requirements are straightforward and should not be too intimidating. Take a moment to clearly understand the applications process now to avoid undue stress later.

The Application Form

Most of the private schools in Houston post application forms to each school's individual website, while a few private schools release paper applications upon request. As with colleges, private schools require an application fee (usually around $100) to be submitted along with the application form. The fee is non-refundable. Depending on the grade to which the student is applying, the application is filled out by the parent/guardian in regards to the student's information, while the student fills out a questionnaire and/or writes an essay in response to a prompt found on the application. Although the format of the application form varies from school to school, the information required is generally:

- To which grade is the student applying
- Applicant's date of birth and gender
- Applicant's address and contact information
- Status of the applicant's family structure (lives with both parents, parents are divorced, etc.)
- Address and contact information of the applicant's parents/guardians
- Basic information (such as college or occupation) of parents/guardians
- Previous schools attended by the applicant
- Legacy information, if applicable
- Information regarding special circumstances that affected the applicant's previous education (medication, counseling, discipline problems, etc.)
- Applicant's ethnicity and race

Applications will only be reviewed once the student has also submitted the necessary teacher recommendation forms and release forms for transcripts, school records, and health records from the applicant's previous schools.

Teacher Recommendation Form

Students applying to Pre-Kindergarten through Grade 5 must submit a Teacher Recommendation Form from a current teacher, while students applying to Grades 6 to 12 must submit English and Math Teacher Recommendation Forms. Some private schools require a Counselor/Principal Recommendation Form or a Special Interest Recommendation Form for upper grades. Each teacher recommendation form is confidential and parents and students are not allowed to view the completed form. Teacher Recommendation Forms paint a picture of the applicant's abilities as a student and as an individual:

- Pre-K and Kindergarten—detailed information regarding the student's social skills and physical development, such as how the student works in large groups and the student's spatial awareness
- Grades 1 to 5—detailed information regarding the student's academic, communication, and social skills in the classroom
- English and Math—detailed information regarding the student's academic, communication, and social skills in each subject
- Counselor/Principal—detailed information regarding the student's academic and social skills in and out of the classroom
- Special Interest—acts as a reference form, which details the student's abilities, character, and leadership skills in the activity with which the reference is familiar

The teacher recommendation forms will also provide information regarding the student's behavioral tendencies in the classroom, such as tardiness, aggression, and study habits. The only portion of the form filled out by the applicant's parent/guardian is the student's name and the list of schools to which the student is applying.

Standardized Testing

All private schools require applicants to submit results from specific standardized tests as part of the application process. The standardized tests are designed to test the ability and knowledge of each student and to demonstrate to the school the applicant's mastery of the material. Testing normally occurs at the school to which the student is applying. Private schools prefer that testing occur on their grounds, but will approve testing with an outside source with legitimate credentials and a licensed agent proctoring the test.

Students should prepare well for ISEE and HSPT exams as they are scored relative to the peer-testing group; we discuss preparation for these exams in the next section. Conversely, there is very little that students can do to prepare for the OLSAT, WPPSI, and WISC exams, as these are primarily IQ tests and do not measure a student's previous academic achievements.

- **ISEE** – Independent School Entrance Exam
  - Five part test: Verbal Reasoning, Quantitative Reasoning, Reading Comprehension, Mathematics Achievement, and Essay
  - Wrong answers are not counted against the student's score
  - The Essay is not scored but is sent to each school for review

- **HSPT** – High School Placement Test
  - Five part test: Verbal Skills, Quantitative Skills, Reading, Mathematics, and Language Skills
  - Wrong answers are not counted against the student's score
  - May also include a Mechanical Aptitude, Science, or Catholic Religion test

- **OLSAT** – Otis-Lennon School Ability Test
  - Assesses a student's Verbal and Non-Verbal abilities
  - Verbal Comprehension: Antonyms, Sentence Completion, Sentence Arrangement
  - Verbal Reasoning: Arithmetic Reasoning, Logical Selection, Word/Letter Matrix, Verbal Analogies, Verbal Classification Inference
  - Figural Reasoning: Figural Analogies, Pattern Matrix, Figural Series
  - Quantitative Reasoning: Number Series, Numeric Inference, Number Matrix

- **WPPSI** – Wechsler Preschool and Primary Scale of Intelligence
  - IQ test for students of 2 ½ to 7 years of age
  - The student answers questions in each subtest until the student incorrectly answers three questions in a row
  - Consists of 14 subtests: Block Design, Information, Matrix Reasoning, Vocabulary, Picture Concepts, Symbol Search, Word Reasoning, Coding, Comprehension, Picture Completion, Similarities, Receptive Vocabulary, Object Assembly, Picture Naming

- **WISC** – Wechsler Intelligence Scale for Children
  - o IQ test for students between 6 and 16 years of age
  - o The full IQ score is determined from four composite scores: VCI, PRI, PSI, and WMI
  - o Vocabulary Comprehension Index (VCI): Vocabulary, Similarities, Comprehension, Information, and Word Reasoning
  - o Perceptual Reasoning Index (PRI): Block Design, Picture Concepts, Matrix Reasoning, and Picture Completion
  - o Processing Speed Index (PSI): Coding, Symbol Search, and Cancellation
  - o Working Memory Index (WMI): Digital Span, Letter-Numbering Sequencing, and Arithmetic

Catholic high schools for boys generally require the HSPT and Catholic high schools for girls generally require the ISEE. Other private schools in Houston require the ISEE. For schools that require it, the IQ test that the school selects is based on age.

Transcripts and Records

Applicants must release any and all records to the private schools to which they are applying. These records include official school transcripts, test scores, and health records. Generally, the transcript should reflect the last two academic years as well as the applicant's current fall semester.

Get to Know the School – Shadowing, Tours, and Open Houses

The application process is an exchange of information between the student, the parents/guardians, and the school. While the application form and the student interview paints a picture of the applicant for the school, events such as "shadowing," tours, and open houses paint a picture of the school for the student. These opportunities should be seized upon to fully prepare the student to choose which schools to apply.

In the professional world, newly hired employees will "shadow" or follow one of the company's veteran employees to get a feel for their new job and the job's environment. The same is true for private schools. Depending on the school, the applicant will "shadow" a faculty member during various stages of the application process to get a glimpse of the school's environment and operational practices. Generally, parents/guardians are not included in the "shadowing" process. The applicant might also be paired with a volunteer student to be shown around the school. The applicant might observe or participate in a classroom in action, be given a tour of the school's facilities, meet with other faculty members, and/or be introduced to clubs and organizations hosted by the school.

Tours and Open Houses are also important in determining to which schools a student should apply. The parents/guardians and the applicant will experience the school firsthand and meet with the faculty and administrators who would oversee the applicant's education. Tours might include focal points such as the school's classrooms, athletics facilities, libraries, and science labs, much like when a student participates in "shadowing."

The Student Interview

The ultimate goal of the student interview is for the school to personally see what kind of student the applicant is and what characteristics the applicant might bring to the school. Private schools do not release exact details on the questions asked during student interviews to prevent parents/guardians from conditioning the applicant. However, preparations can be made so that students are ready for any and all questions sent their way (similar to preparing for job interview):

- Display confidence—the applicant should speak clearly and confidently; firm handshake
- Maintain direct eye contact—direct eye contact shows the interviewer that the student is paying attention; straying eyes show anxiety or indifference
- Research—the applicant should know as much information about the school as possible

Student Practice interview questions:

- Why did you choose this school?
- What do you expect to get out of your education here?
- How have your extracurricular activities influenced you?
- What clubs/organizations are you interested in joining?
- What are your career goals?
- What are your life's ambitions?
- Where have you traveled and what were your experiences like?

This is one of those intentionally left blank pages. If it weren't blank, the next page would be on the wrong side of a double-sided page!

Standardized Tests Preparation
ISEE & HSPT

Potential private school high school students will likely be required to take the ISEE and/or HSPT standardized entrance exams. Similar to the SAT and ACT for college, these examinations test student's ability to learn and their past achievements. Students should prepare well for these exams as scores are calculated relative to the peer-testing group. Students typically take these tests in early January at their first choice schools.

The Independent School Entrance Exam (ISEE)

The Education Records Bureau's (ERB) ISEE features three levels: Lower Level (Applicants to 5th and 6th grade), Middle Level (Applicants to 7th and 8th grade), and Upper Level (Applicants to 9th, 10th, 11th, and 12th grade). The structure of each test is the same. However, time limitations and the difficulty of the material are dependent on the level of the test and are grade-level appropriate. The first four sections are multiple-choice with four answer choices for each question. The Essay is not scored, but it is sent to all schools designated by the student on the registration form. The Verbal and Quantitative Reasoning sections test a student's abstract reasoning skills while the Reading Comprehension and Mathematics Achievement sections test a student's content knowledge.

Structure of the ISEE (Upper Level)

Test Section	Time Limit	Content Area / Skills	# Questions
Verbal Reasoning	20 Minutes	Synonyms Sentence Completions TOTAL	40 Questions
Quantitative Reasoning	35 Minutes	Arithmetic/Algebra/Geometry Concepts/Understanding Applications/Higher-Order Thinking Quantitative Comparison TOTAL	37 Questions
Reading Comprehension	40 Minutes	Humanities Science Social Studies TOTAL	36 Questions
Mathematics Achievement	40 Minutes	Knowledge and Skills Computation / Comprehension Arithmetic/Algebra/Geometry Applications TOTAL	47 Questions
Essay	30 Minutes		1 Prompt

What to Expect on the ISEE

The Verbal Reasoning section tests the student's ability with vocabulary and vocabulary application. The first twenty questions are Synonyms questions that require the student to not only know the definition of the capitalized vocabulary word but also the definitions of each answer choice. The last twenty questions are Sentence Completion questions that test the student's ability to apply one's knowledge of vocabulary in the context of a sentence. The sentence will have either one or two blanks and the student must select the answer choice that best fits into those blanks.

The Quantitative Reasoning section, perhaps the most difficult, also features two parts: word problems and quantitative comparison questions. The questions in both sections vary in amount of work, regularly requiring little to no actual calculations in order to answer the question. The student is tested on one's ability to reason through information and one's comprehension of math theorems and rules. The quantitative comparison questions present two quantities and ask the student to determine the quantities' relationship to one another (or if it can even be determined).

The Reading Comprehension section features passages from various fields and subjects, including pieces on scientific concepts, historical information, and poetry. The questions following each passage include main idea, supporting idea, inference, vocabulary, organization/logic, and tone/style/figurative language questions. These questions test the student's ability to understand themes and concepts within each passage, know definitions of words within a particular context, and to draw conclusions from content not explicitly stated in the passage.

The Mathematics Achievement section tests a student's ability to solve questions concerning Numbers and Operations, Algebra, Geometry, Measurement, Data Analysis and Probability, and Problem Solving (according to standards by the National Council of Teachers of Mathematics). As opposed to the Quantitative Reasoning section, students may need to do calculations to solve the questions in the Mathematics Achievement section and students will need to be familiar with mathematical terminology. For measurement conversions, students do not need to have memorized conversions in the U. S. standard system. Conversions are normally given in questions that require them, but conversions within the same unit in the metric system are not.

The Essay gives a student the chance to demonstrate to the schools how well the student can organize one's thoughts and convey an argument or statement within a short essay in response to a prompt. The prompt is grade-level appropriate, and the student will be able to answer the prompt pulling from one's experiences and education. The student will have two pages of lined paper on which to write the essay and must use an ink pen. The student may write the essay in cursive or print.

ISEE Highlights

- 1 point is awarded for each correct answer in all sections
- There are no deductions for incorrect answers in all sections (answer all questions!)
- The student is not allowed a calculator for the math sections
- Students are not provided scratch paper—all work is to be done on the test booklet
- Students may only take the ISEE once every six-months

- Students must take the ISEE at an approved testing facility with a licensed ISEE proctor
  - Generally the student will take the ISEE at the student's most desired school
- The ISEE features four scores:
  - Raw score – the total number of correct answers in each section
  - Scaled score – a reflection of the raw score in a scaled format from 760 to 940
    - The ERB uses various versions of the ISEE each year and the scaled score has the same meaning across all versions of the test, as opposed to the raw score
  - Percentile rank – the student's standing in comparison to the norm group
    - Percentile ranks range from 1 to 99. A percentile rank of 75 in Verbal Reasoning would mean the student scored better than 75 percent of the norm group
    - The norm group is all students in independent schools in the same grade who took the ISEE over the last three years throughout the nation
  - Stanine score – ranging from 1 to 9, stanines reflect segments of the percentile rank
    - Stanine of 1 to 5 reflects percentile ranks 1 to 59
    - Stanine of 6 reflects percentile ranks 60 to 76
    - Stanine of 7 reflects percentile ranks 77 to 88
    - Stanine of 8 reflects percentile ranks 89 to 95
    - Stanine of 9 reflects percentile ranks 96 to 99

The High School Placement Test (HSPT)

Scholastic Testing Service's HSPT is an admissions test for entry into Catholic High Schools. The HSPT contains five multiple-choice sections: Verbal, Quantitative Skills, Reading, Mathematics, and Language Skills. Depending on the school, the HSPT might also feature an optional section covering Science, Mechanical Aptitude or Catholic Religion. The optional test is not included in the composite score from the HSPT and not every school chooses to use the optional test. Schools that require the optional test might use the score to determine a student's placement in particular courses such as honors and advanced classes.

Structure of the HSPT

Test Section	Time Limit	Content Area / Skills	# Questions
Verbal Skills	16 Minutes	Verbal Analogies	10 Questions
		Synonyms	15 Questions
		Logic	10 Questions
		Verbal Classifications	16 Questions
		Antonyms	9 Questions
		TOTAL	60 Questions
Quantitative Skills	30 Minutes	Number Series	18 Questions
		Geometric Comparison	9 Questions
		Non-Geometric Comparison	8 Questions
		Number Manipulation	17 Questions
		TOTAL	52 Questions
Reading	25 Minutes	Comprehension	40 Questions
		Vocabulary	22 Questions
		TOTAL	62 Questions
Mathematics	45 Minutes	Concepts	24 Questions
		Problem-Solving	40 Questions
		TOTAL	64 Questions
Language Skills	25 Minutes	Punctuation and Capitalization	12 Questions
		Usage	28 Questions
		Spelling	10 Questions
		Composition	10 Questions
		TOTAL	60 Questions

What to Expect on the HSPT

The Verbal Skills section tests a student's ability to answer verbal analogy, synonym, logic, verbal classification, and antonym questions. Verbal analogies address whether a student understands a relationship between two words (ex. Tree is to limb as human is to arm—whole to part). The Synonym and Antonym questions test the student's knowledge of vocabulary, including the definitions of the answer choices. In verbal classifications, students are asked to identify which of one or four answer choices does not belong with the others. In logic questions, students are given three statements and students must determine if the third statement is true, false, or uncertain based on the truth of the first two statements.

The Quantitative Skills section tests a student's ability to answer number series, geometric comparison, non-geometric comparison, and number manipulation questions. Number series questions test a student's ability to determine the relationship between numbers, letters, and/or symbols in a sequence. Geometric and Non-Geometric Comparison questions ask students to compare three figures/shapes (geometric) or numerical/mathematical expressions (non-geometric) and determine the relationship between them. In number manipulation questions, students must use multiple mathematical steps to solve each problem (ex. What number is 3 more than 1/3 of 200).

The Reading section contains passages that test a student's comprehension of ideas, themes, tone, and the author's intent. The student must be able to quickly grasp the main idea of the passage, understand the supporting details within the passage, and must demonstrate knowledge of vocabulary within the context of the passage. The passages will cover a wide variety of subjects, including science, history, literature, and societal topics.

The Mathematics section tests a student's ability to answer questions concerning arithmetic, algebra, and geometry appropriate to eighth grade students. In arithmetic, students must demonstrate familiarity with the number line, order of operations, multiplication, division, addition, subtraction, fractions, decimals, percentages and other aspects of basic math. Students will solve questions involving algebraic equations and concepts such as absolute value. In geometry, students will need to show their understanding of area of plane figures, perimeter of plan figures, volume of solid figures, angles, and coordinate geometry (graphing). Students will also be solving word problems that feature rate, time, distance, and work problems (two or more workers performing at different rates).

The Language Skills section tests a student's knowledge of grammar and writing mechanics. Students will answer questions involving spelling, punctuation and capitalization, principles of grammar, and language composition and expression. Topic development questions will either give the student a topic sentence and the student must choose a second and third sentence that best develops that topic or the student will be given a title and the student must choose a topic sentence or relative sentence that belongs under that title. Sentence appropriateness questions ask a student to identify whether a sentence belongs with the others or what the best placement for a sentence would be.

HSPT Highlights

- 1 point is awarded for each correct answer in all sections
- There are no deductions for incorrect answers in all sections (answer all questions!)
- The student is not allowed a calculator for the math sections
- Students are not provided scratch paper—all work is to be done on the test booklet
- The student will take the HSPT at the Catholic high school they would most prefer to attend, though the student may list other Catholic high schools to be sent the student's HSPT scores
- The HSPT features multiple scores:
  - Raw score – the total number of correct answers in each section
  - Scaled score – each raw score is converted into a scaled score of 200 to 800

- Like the ISEE, Scholastic Testing Service uses various versions of the HSPT to test students, and the scaled scores mean the same thing across all versions
- Percentile rank – the student's standing in comparison to the national sample
  - Each section receives a percentile rank
  - Scholastic Testing Service also provides a local percentile rank
  - Each percentile rank is followed by a stanine, which represents the percentile rank in a score of 1 to 9
- Cognitive Skills – collection of scores and a total from the Verbal and Quantitative Skills sections; includes the CSQ, scaled scores, percentile ranks, and stanines
- Basic Skills – collection of scores and a total from the Reading, Mathematics, and Language Skills sections; includes scaled scores, percentile ranks, and stanines
- Composite – combined scaled score, percentile rank, and stanine from all five sections (does not include the optional test)
- Optional Test – national percentile rank of the optional test: Mechanical Aptitude, Science, or Catholic Religion
- Cognitive Skills Quotient (CSQ) – similar to an IQ score with an operational range of 55 to 145, this score reflects the student's learning potential and is based on age
- Grade Equivalent (GE) – demonstrates the student's aptitude in terms of scoring similarly to a student in a higher grade (ex. GE of 11.5 means the student is scoring as an 11th grader in the fifth month of the academic year would)

The ISEE vs. the HSPT

Even in middle school, a student's time might not wholly be one's own. Preparing for two exams could hinder the student's schoolwork and extracurricular activities. The question then boils down to: "With limited time, which test should the student focus one's attention?" Rumor might suggest that the ISEE is the more difficult test of the two. In essence, the ISEE and HSPT cover much of the same material, thus the student might prepare for both tests by focusing on a single exam. However, the ISEE and HSPT present the material in different ways that might affect the student's ability to answer the questions. A student might do well in answering quantitative comparison questions on the ISEE, but is given pause when faced with geometric and non-geometric comparison questions on the HSPT.

Parents should take into consideration which schools the student wants to attend and determine which exam each school requires for the admissions process. If the student only wants to attend Catholic high schools, then the question might already be answered. However, certain Catholic high schools require the ISEE instead of the HSPT, and the competitive nature of private schools might require the student to take both exams to safeguard the student's education at a private high school.

Students should first become familiar with the material and types of questions each exam contains by taking an ISEE and an HSPT cold (no preparation) from start to finish under the correct time limitations. Afterwards, parents should highlight the student's weakest areas and compare each exam for similarities in weaknesses. Once the student's weaknesses are discovered, the student can prepare appropriately by focusing on these weaknesses through self-practice, working with a tutor, and/or enrolling in an ISEE or HSPT preparation course.

When preparing for either test, students must remember that standardized test strategies alone will not help one score well. The student must fully understand the concepts addressed by either test, just as it is in the classroom when preparing for a midterm exam or the final exam. Guess work might lead students to the correct answer, but it will not effectively support them as they continue their academic careers.

School Profiles and Summary Data

In this section, we profile thirty-eight private and select public middle and high schools; elementary schools are included only when the school as a whole also offers a middle or high school. The information displayed in this section was culled from school websites, marketing materials, administrators, parents, students, and third party sources such as the US Government and National Merit Scholarship Corporation. We made every attempt to ensure the accuracy of the data including asking each school to validate their profiles. When in doubt, parents should independently verify this information.

General Academic, Inc.

Index of Profiled Schools

School	Map #	Page #		Map #	Page #
Alexander Smith	1	78	Pin Oak MS*	20	136
Annunciation Orthodox	2	81	Post Oak Montessori	21	139
Awty International	3	84	Presbyterian School	22	142
Bellaire HS*	4	87	River Oaks Baptist School	23	144
Beren Academy	5	91	School of the Woods	24	149
Briarwood School	6	93	Second Baptist	25	155
British School	7	96	St. Agnes	26/35	155
Carnegie Vanguard HS*	8	99	St. Catherine's Montessori	27	159
DeBakey HS*	9	102	St. Francis Episcopal Day	28	162
Duchesne	10	105	St. John's	29	165
Emery/Weiner	11	109	St. Mark's Episcopal	30	169
Episcopal High School	12	112	St. Pius X	31	172
Houston Christian HS	13	115	St. Stephen's Episcopal	32	175
HSPVA*	14	118	St. Thomas Episcopal	33	178
Incarnate Word Academy	15	121	St. Thomas High School	34	181
Kinkaid	16	124	Strake Jesuit	35/26	184
Lamar HS*	17	127	TH Rogers*	36	187
Lanier MS*	18	130	The Village School	37	190
Pershing MS*	19	133	Westchester Academy*	38	193

Indicates a public school.

A Note About the Maps

Maps created using Google Maps.
You can view an interactive version online at: http://g.co/maps/xjg53

A Note About the Profiles

We have made every effort to ensure that the information presented in these profiles is accurate. However, please know that information such as dates, tuition, and fees are always subject to change after this book was compiled and distributed. When in doubt, please contact the school directly to verify the information presented.

Wide Area Map (Including Beltway 8)

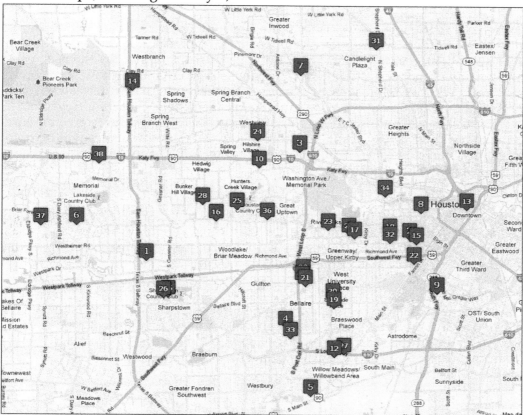

Local Area Map (Including I-610)

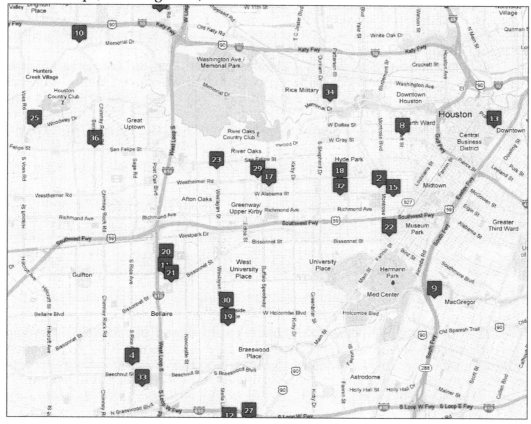

About the Numbers and Fast Facts

Over the next few pages, we present more than fifteen sets of data about the thirty-eight schools profiled in this book. We present this information not as a way to rank schools but rather as another component of a very large picture. By themselves, these numbers likely do not accurately reflect a school's performance or how well your child will or will not thrive in a particular environment. In particular, some of these statistics have correlative errors; for example, is the school's teaching responsible for how well students do on a standardized test such as the SAT or were the enrolled students naturally excellent test takers to begin with? These statistics will help you to build a fuller image of a school, but please do not let them be the only or even the most important characteristic that you weigh.

School Type/ Affiliation
The type of school or its affiliation has the potential to quickly say a lot about how a school is organized or how it operates including religious beliefs and teaching methodology. Nearly 70% of the private schools profiled here are religiously affiliated, and over half of this group is Catholic.

Date Founded
The founding date has the potential to provide insight into how established a school's practices are and its relative levels of prestige. Very established schools may be steeped in tradition that add to a school's allure. Conversely, old and rigid rules and customs may also be unattractive for some families. The average age for schools profiled here is just fifty-six years.

Grades Served
Of particular importance for private schools, the presence of more grades could mean fewer application processes for parents. Imagine having to only go through the admissions process one time until college! There are twelve schools of this group that offer a curriculum beginning in pre-kindergarten and extending through twelfth grade.

Enrollment (Total)
The overall size of a school can say a lot about the experience and curriculum offerings. Larger schools tend to offer more extracurricular activities, athletic teams, arts classes, and electives because they have the economies of scale that smaller schools do not enjoy. However, some students may prefer smaller, cozier environments where everybody knows everybody. The public schools profiled in this book are more than 30% larger than private schools on average; this size difference disregards the number of grades offered.

Enrollment (Highest Grade)
This number provides a more precise picture versus total enrollment in that it removes the variable of number of grades a school serves. Comparing highest offered grades (i.e. 12 for high schools, 8 for middle schools), the difference in size between public and private schools increases dramatically. On average, a public school grade is more than five times as large as its private school counterpart—433 students for a public school versus 79 for a private school.

Campus Size
A larger campus usually affords more athletic and recreational facilities. A few acres are the difference between a campus that feels like a miniature Rice versus one that feels like a miniature Galleria. Larger campuses tend to be further away from the city center. Private schools have almost twice as much land space than public schools.

Students Per Acre

Also relating to campus size, this number is a more precise measurement of density. Public schools are approximately four times as dense as private schools. Higher numbers usually indicate that a school has more tall buildings with less green space, while lower numbers indicate shorter buildings with more green space.

Endowment

Big endowments often allow schools to subsidize the cost of a student's education. This subsidy does not usually mean that most parents pay less tuition, rather it means that a well-endowed school may be able to offer more versus a tuition driven school at the same cost; more being smaller classes, more extracurricular activities, electives, and the like. Big endowments may also allow a school to admit more students on financial aid, leading to a more diverse student body. Given the young age of most of the schools in Houston, sizeable endowments are usually hard to come by. Most schools do not make endowment information readily available to the public. It's a safe bet that if a school's endowment isn't publicized, it's because there's not much of one.

Student to Teacher Ratio

Fewer students per teacher usually results in a student benefiting from more individualized attention. A teacher with just 9 students in their class has the ability to adapt and customize their curriculum much more than one that has to contend with 25 or more. More teachers may also mean that a school can offer a broader curriculum, which includes more electives or a broader range of core subject classes. Public schools have approximately 40% larger classes; Catholic schools fall between non-Catholic private and public schools.

Minority Enrollment

This number is a measurement of diversity. According to the 2010 US Census demographic data on Harris County—the county which comprises most of Houston—56.6% is "white," 18.9% is "black," .7% is "American Indian and Alaska Native," 6.2% is "Asian," .1% is "Native Hawaiian and Other Pacific Islander," 3.2% is "reporting two or more races," 40.8% "Hispanic or Latino origin," and 33% "White persons not Hispanic" (adds up to more than 100% due to how the Census collects data). Public schools have almost a 100% more diverse population than the average private school. Catholic schools fall between non-Catholic private and public schools. A handful of private middle schools do not release demographic information about their students.

Foreign Languages

The study of foreign language allows students to broaden their cultural horizons and learn a truly life-long skill that opens the door to foreign worlds and even increased career opportunities. Of the schools profiled here, every one offers Spanish except for the Briarwood School, which does not offer any foreign languages. French is the next most popular language (29/38), followed by Latin (20/38), Chinese Mandarin (18/38), Italian (13/38), German (7/38), Greek (6/38), and Hebrew (3/38). Note that this count includes five IB schools. IB schools technically offer all of the languages above except Hebrew. However, IB schools may not have an instructor on staff that can teach every language offered in the IB curriculum, in which case the student will be advised to take a more common language or enroll through a remote learning platform.

AP/ IB Classes

Advanced Placement and International Baccalaureate (IB) classes allow gifted and talented students to better maximize their full potential through more challenging coursework. Note that schools that offer the IB program must technically offer all of the IB curriculum's more than fifty courses. However, most schools do not have enough students to field a class in all courses. When students insist on taking a course that is not regularly offered, they are usually allowed to participate in a computer based or self-guided course. Public schools offer approximately 20% more advanced classes than their private school counterparts; Catholic schools offered fewer AP or IB classes than both public and private schools.

Interscholastic Sports
More sports teams usually means more opportunities for students of varying ages to get involved in a wider range of competitive sports. Larger schools tend to field more sports teams at different levels of competitiveness such as intramural, junior varsity, and varsity. Most schools offer between 7 and 10 interscholastic sports teams. Note that some schools offer intramural and "freshman only" teams that allow more students to participate at varying levels of competitiveness; these non-"school vs. school" teams are not included in this count.

National Merit Semi-Finalists (Number)
This number is a count of eleventh graders who scored in the top 1% on the PSAT as administered by the National Merit Scholarship Corporation in October of 2010. St. John's and Bellaire HS boast of almost ten times more of these awarded students than any other school.

National Merit Semi-Finalists (Percent)
This value provides an arguably better representation versus the actual count in that it takes into account class size. When taken as a percentage, St. John's retains its nearly ten-fold lead over other schools. Note that the national average is 1%.

A Note on College Preparedness and the National Merit® Scholarship
With relatively few hard numbers by which to compare schools, parents may be tempted to look at figures such as "average SAT scores," "college acceptances," and number of "National Merit Semi-Finalists." However, parents should use caution—these data points are admittedly good at describing the profile of a single class, but it's difficult to verifiably say that there is a direct causal relationship between these college fitness numbers and the quality of the school's education.

Many of General Academic's most academically talented students were already scoring in the top 1% on their SATs even before they entered high school (many 7th graders take the SAT and/or ACT as part of the Duke University Talent Identification Program). Furthermore, a list of colleges to where graduates have been accepted in the last five years is similarly spurious. For example, if a graduating class has 200 students and one of those students was admitted to Rice or Harvard or MIT, does that mean everyone else got in too? These lists really say very little.

In general, General Academic believes that most if not all of the schools here offer programs that will more than adequately prepare any student for a demanding college education; however, it is up to the individual student to a) take advantage of those opportunities and b) apply those skills judiciously to future studies in college.

These numbers may, however, accurately indicate that a quorum of academic elite students has decided to attend a certain high school. What these statistics indicate then is that if parents want to be among this elite, they may want to follow in the same path.

One of the most widely espoused figures schools will use is the number of National Merit Semi-Finalists their junior class had in the annual National Merit Scholarship Competition. This competition takes place annually every fall for high school juniors. Juniors compete by sitting for the Practice SAT (PSAT), which is an abbreviated SAT. Semi-Finalists represent the approximate top 1% of test takers. The cut-off score to obtain this designation in Texas in the 2010-2011 Competition was a 215, which translates into an SAT score of 2150.

National Merit Semi-Finalists generally qualify for scholarships that can range from full tuition at certain public colleges to $5,000 and $10,000 scholarships at prestigious, private universities.

Tuition

Private school is expensive; public school is free. This number does not include private school fees that often add up to thousands of dollars on top of the tuition. Big fees often exceeding $500 include new student enrollment, books, technology, and class trips. For a small fee, most schools allow tuition to be paid over the course of a school year in regular installments. Regardless of grade level, private school tuition will set most families back nearly $18,000 a year. Catholic school tuition is nearly 25% lower than non-Catholic schools.

General Academic, Inc.

Summary Data

School	School Type	Date Founded	Grades Served	Enrollment (Total)	Enrollment (Highest Grade)	Campus Size (Acres)	Students per Acre	Endowment	Student to Teacher Ratio	Minorities	AP/ IB Classes	Languages Offered	Interscholastic Sports Teams	National Merit Semi Finalists	Tuition (Highest Grade)
Alexander Smith	Independent	1968	9th-12	50	18	<1	50	None	4:1	15%	4 AP	S	N/A	0%	$26,600
Annunciation Orthodox	Greek	1970	PreK-8	673	73	3.7	181.9	N/A	11:1	15%	N/A	GK, S	9	N/A	$18,135
Awty International	International	1956	PreK-12	1206	84	15	80.4	$4M	7:1	33%	52 IB	IB	8	1%	$20,472
Bellaire HS	Public Magnet	1955	9th-12	3377	706	7	482.4	None	18:1	67%	22	IB	12	5%	N/A
Beren Academy	Jewish	1969	PreK-12	300	19	55	5.5	N/A	5:1	21%	12	H	4	0%	$18,883
Briarwood School	Special Needs	1967	K-12	300	45	9.2	32.6	N/A	8:1	12%	N/A	0	8	0%	$17,250
British School	International	2000	PreK-12	521	21	14	37.2	None	11:1	14%	N/A	IB	7	0%	$23,070
Carnegie Vanguard HS	Public Magnet	2002	9th-12	524	84	6	87.3	None	15:1	56%	20	A, C, F, L, S	2	2%	N/A
DeBakey HS	Public Magnet	1972	9th-12	887	189	N/A	N/A	None	16:1	92%	15	F, S	0	4%	N/A
Duchesne	Catholic, Girls	1960	PreK-12	714	67	~14	51	$6M	8:1	25%	16 AP	F, S, L	10	3%	$20,047
Emery/Weiner	Jewish	1978	6th-12	479	60	12	39.9	$10M	6:1	4%	N/A	H, S, L	10	1%	$20,725
Episcopal High School	Episcopal	1983	9th-12	664	163	35	19	$25M	7:1	16%	15 AP	C, F, L, S	16	3%	$20,385
Houston Christian HS	Christian	1997	9th-12	485	113	45	10.8	N/A	9:1	20%	18	C, L, S	13	4%	$17,430
HSPVA	Public Magnet	1971	9th-12	654	151	N/A	654	None	16:1	49%	9	F, S	0	1%	N/A
Incarnate Word Academy	Catholic, Girls	1873	9th-12	262	55	<1	262	N/A	9:1	65%	6 AP	F, L, S	9	0%	$9,600
Kinkaid	Independent	1906	PreK-12	1366	136	65	21	$79M	18:1	23%	14 AP	C, F, L, S	15	7%	$20,530
Lamar HS	Public Magnet	1936	9th-12	3003	650	25.67	117	None	18:1	66%	30 IB	IB	15	1%	N/A
Lanier MS	Public Magnet	1926	6th-8	1347	422	N/A	N/A	None	18:1	58%	N/A	C, F, G, S	11	N/A	N/A
Pershing MS	Public Magnet	1928	6th-8	1748	597	N/A	N/A	None	17:1	81%	N/A	C, F, S	10	N/A	N/A

School	Type	Founded						Ratio	%	AP	Languages		%	Tuition
Pin Oak MS	Public Magnet	2002	1153	362	18	64.1	None	17:01	68%	N/A	C, F, L, H, I, S	9	N/A	N/A
Post Oak Montessori	Montessori	1963	353	9	3.44	102.6	N/A	9:1	25%	N/A	C, S	3	N/A	$21,000
Presbyterian School	Presbyterian	1988	512	53	16	N/A	N/A	8:1	12%	N/A	S	10	N/A	$18,770
River Oaks Baptist	Baptist	1955	789	75	N/A	N/A	N/A	15:1	NP	N/A	S	10	N/A	$19,820
School of the Woods	Montessori	1962	378	21	5	75.6	N/A	8:1	22%	N/A	F, S, ASL	4	0%	$17,280
Second Baptist	Baptist	1946	1122	66	42	26.7	N/A	9:1	NP	N/A	F, S	11	3%	$16,584
St. Agnes	Catholic, Girls	1906	874	208	15.6	56	N/A	13:1	39%	12 AP	C, F, L, S	12	3%	$14,550
St. Catherine's	Montessori	1966	155	10	7.4	20.9	N/A	10:1	52%	N/A	S	4	N/A	$10,720
St. Francis Episcopal Day	Episcopal	1952	645	71	15.5	41.6	NP	7:1	20%	N/A	S	10	N/A	$19,960
St. Johns	Independent	1946	1249	132	28	44.6	$59M	7:1	19%	17 AP	C, F, L, S	14	35%	$20,235
St. Mark's Episcopal	Episcopal	1960	383	36	NP	NP	NP	13:1	30%	N/A	S	4	N/A	$15,748
St. Pius X	Catholic	1956	695	155	24	N/A	N/A	14:1	53%	10 AP	F, I, S, L	12	0%	$11,700
St. Stephen's Episcopal	Montessori	1971	190	13	N/A	N/A	N/A	6:1	18%	N/A	S, F	5	0%	$16,140
St. Thomas Episcopal	Episcopal	1955	628	44	N/A	N/A	N/A	9:1	34%	15 AP	C, F, L, S	8	5%	$13,533
St. Thomas High School	Catholic, Boys	1900	709	170	N/A	N/A	N/A	12:1	35%	10	F, L, S	13	1%	$13,250
Strake Jesuit	Catholic, Boys	1960	906	218	44	20.6	N/A	12:1	37%	12	C, F, L, S	13	5%	$15,150
TH Rogers	Public Magnet	1962	396	122	NP	NP	None	10:1	74%	N/A	C, F, S	7	N/A	N/A
The Village School	Independent	1966	788	51*	18	43.8	None	9:1	55%	N/A	IB	11	4%	$20,925
Westchester Academy	Public Charter	1967	977	136	8	122.1	None	13:1	64%	14	F, G, I, S	0	1%	N/A

Foreign Language Abbreviations

C = Chinese, F = French, G = German, GK= Greek, L = Latin, H = Hebrew, I = Italian, S = Spanish, IB = International Baccalaureate Languages, ASL = American

Private Schools by Affiliation	
1	Baptist
River Oaks Baptist School	
Second Baptist	
2	Catholic Co-Ed
St. Catherine's Montessori	
St. Pius X	
2	Catholic Boys
Strake Jesuit	
St. Thomas High School	
3	Catholic Girls
Duchesne	
St. Agnes	
Incarnate Word Academy	
1	Christian
Houston Christian HS	
5	Episcopal
Episcopal High School	
St. Francis Episcopal Day	
St. Mark's Episcopal School	
St. Stephen's Episcopal	
St. Thomas Episcopal	
1	Greek
Annunciation Orthodox	
4	Independent
Alexander Smith	
Kinkaid	
St. Johns	
Village School	
2	International
Awty International	
British School	
2	Jewish
Beren Academy	
Emery/ Weiner	
4	Montessori
Post Oak Montessori School	
School of the Woods	
St. Catherine's Montessori	
St. Stephen's Episcopal	
1	Presbyterian
Presbyterian School	
1	Special Needs
Briarwood School	

Private Schools by Grade Level	
12	PreK-12
Awty International	
Beren Academy	
British School	
Duchesne	
Kinkaid	
Post Oak Montessori School	
School of the Woods	
Second Baptist	
St. Stephen's Episcopal	
St. Thomas Episcopal	
The Village School	
5	PreK-8/9
Annunciation Orthodox	
Presbyterian School	
River Oaks Baptist School	
St. Catherine's Montessori	
St. Francis Episcopal Day	
2	K-12
St. John's	
Briarwood School	
	6-12
Emery/ Weiner	
8	9-12
Alexander Smith	
Episcopal High School	
Houston Christian HS	
Incarnate Word Academy	
St. Agnes	
St. Pius X	
St. Thomas High School	
Strake Jesuit	

Date Founded		
1	Incarnate Word Academy	1873
2	St. Thomas High School	1900
3	Kinkaid	1906
4	St. Agnes	1906
5	Lanier MS	1926
6	Pershing MS	1928
7	Lamar HS	1936
8	St. Johns	1946
	Average All Profiled Schools	**1956**

Endowment		
1	Kinkaid	$79M
2	St. Johns	$59M
3	Episcopal High School	$25M
4	Emery/Weiner	$10M
5	Duchesne	$6M
6	Awty International	$4M
	Average Among Reporting Schools	$29M

Enrollment (Total)		
1	Bellaire HS	3377
2	Lamar HS	3003
3	Pershing MS	1748
4	Kinkaid	1366
5	Lanier MS	1347
6	St. Johns	1249
7	Awty International	1206
8	Pin Oak MS	1153
	Average All Profiled Schools	828
	Average Profiled Private Schools	622
	Average Profiled Public Schools	1406

Enrollment (Highest Grade)		
1	Bellaire HS	706
2	Lamar HS	650
3	Pershing MS	597
4	Lanier MS	422
5	Pin Oak MS	362
6	Strake Jesuit	218
7	St. Agnes	208
8	DeBakey HS	189
	Average All Profiled Schools	174
	Average Profiled Private Schools	79
	Average Profiled Public Schools	433

Campus Size (Acres)		
1	Kinkaid	65
2	Beren Academy	55
3	Houston Christian High School	45
4	Strake Jesuit	44
5	Second Baptist	42
6	Episcopal High School	35
7	St. Johns	28
8	Lamar HS	26
	Average All Profiled Schools	22
	Average Profiled Private Schools	24
	Average Profiled Public Schools	13

Students per Acre		
1	Beren Academy	5.5
2	Houston Christian High School	10.8
3	Episcopal High School	19.0
4	Strake Jesuit	20.6
5	St. Catherine's Montessori	20.9
6	Kinkaid	21.0
7	Second Baptist	26.7
8	Briarwood School	32.6
	Average All Profiled Schools	102
	Average Profiled Private Schools	60
	Average Profiled Public Schools	254

Student to Teacher Ratio	
1 Alexander Smith	4:1
2 Beren Academy	5:1
3 Emery/Weiner	6:1
4 St. Stephen's Episcopal	6:1
5 Episcopal High School	7:1
6 St. Francis Episcopal Day	7:1
7 St. Johns	7:1
8 Awty International	7:1
Average All Profiled Schools	11:1
Average Profiled Private Schools	9:1
Average Profiled Public Schools	16:1
Average Profiled Catholic Schools	11:1

Minority Enrollment (%)	
1 Debakey HS	92%
2 Pershing MS	81%
3 TH Rogers	74%
4 Pin Oak MS	68%
5 Bellaire HS	67%
6 Lamar HS	66%
7 Incarnate Word Academy	65%
8 Westchester Academy	64%
Average All Profiled Schools	38%
Average Profiled Private Schools	27%
Average Profiled Public Schools	68%
Average Profiled Catholic Schools	44%

AP/ IB Classes Offered (#)	
1 Awty International	52
2 Lamar HS	30
3 Bellaire HS	22
4 Carnegie Vanguard HS	20
5 Houston Christian High School	18
6 St. Johns	17
7 Duchesne	16
8 Debakey, Episcopal High School	15
St. Thomas Episcopal	
Average All Profiled Schools	16
Average Excluding IB Schools	13
Average Profiled Private Schools	15
Average Profiled Public Schools	18
Average Profiled Catholic Schools	11

Foreign Languages Offered (#)	
1 Awty International	IB
2 Bellaire HS	IB
3 British School	IB
4 Lamar HS	IB
5 Pin Oak Middle School	6
6 Carnegie Vanguard HS	5
Average All Profiled Schools	7
Average Excluding IB Schools	3
Average Profiled Private Schools	6
Average Profiled Public Schools	12
Average Profiled Catholic Schools	3

Interscholastic Sports Teams (#)	
1	Episcopal High School	16
2	Lamar HS	15
3	Kinkaid	15
4	St. Johns	14
5	St. Thomas High School	13
6	Houston Christian High School	13
7	Strake Jesuit	13
8	Bellaire HS	12
	St. Agnes	
	St. Pius X	
	Average All Profiled Schools	9
	Average Profiled Private Schools	9
	Average Profiled Public Schools	7
	Average Profiled Catholic School	10

Highest Tuition	
1	Alexander Smith	$26,600
2	British School	$23,070
3	Post Oak Montessori School	$21,000
4	The Village School	$20,925
5	Emery/Weiner	$20,725
6	Kinkaid	$20,530
7	Awty International	$20,472
8	Episcopal High School	$20,385
	Average Profiled Private Schools	$17,803
	Average 12th Grade Tuition	$17,873
	Average 8th Grade Tuition	$17,481
	Average Catholic School Tuition	$13,574

National Merit Semi-Finalists (#)	
1	St. Johns	46
2	Bellaire HS	38
3	Strake Jesuit	10
4	Kinkaid	9
5	Debakey HS	8
6	Episcopal High School	7
7	St. Agnes	6
	Average All Profiled Schools	5.3
	Average Profiled Private Schools	4.2
	Average Profiled Public Schools	9
	Average Profiled Catholic School	10.4

National Merit Semi-Finalists (%)	
1	St. Johns	35%
2	Kinkaid	7%
	Bellaire HS	5%
	Emery/ Weiner	5%
	Strake Jesuit	5%
	St. Thomas Episcopal	5%
6	Debakey HS	4%
	The Village School	4%
	Average All Profiled Schools	3.2%
	Average Profiled Private Schools	3.4%
	Average Profiled Public Schools	2.5%
	Average Profiled Catholic School	2%

Alexander Smith Academy

10255 Richmond Avenue, Houston, TX 77042
713-266-0920
www.AlexanderSmith.com

David Arnold, President
Margaret Waldner De La Garza, Principal

Overview

Founded in 1968, David J. Arnold acquired and reincorporated the school in 1973 as a private for-profit company. The school gained full accreditation from the Southern Association of Colleges and Schools in 1976 and from the Texas Education Agency in 1984. Alexander Smith Academy (ASA) stresses its small class size, usually 5-7 students, and individualized attention as its unique selling point.

Religious Affiliation

ASA does not have any religious affiliation.

Location and Facilities

ASA is located near the intersection of Richmond Avenue and the Sam Houston Tollway within a multi-story office building and includes a library. Adjacent properties are also commercial buildings. The school is easily accessible via both the Sam Houston and Westpark Tollways.

Admissions

The admissions process at ASA is straightforward. Interested applicants need only submit the application, current transcript, report cards, and a non-refundable deposit of $300.

Academic Tracks and Curriculum

The school features very small classes, generally between five and seven students. Overall enrollment in grades 9-12 is limited to just 70 students. In spite of its small size, it does offer on-track, honors, and Advanced Placement classes. The ASA school day is primarily Monday through Thursday; Friday is reserved for enrichment tutorials, group workshops, projects, and extra curricular activities.

Students are required to take 24 credits to graduate:

- Ninth Grade: English (Pre-AP), World Geography, Algebra I (Honors), Physical Science, Spanish I, Computer, PE.
- Tenth Grade: English II (Pre-AP), World History, Geometry (Honors), Biology (Honors), Spanish II, Art
- Eleventh Grade: English III (AP), U.S. History (AP), Algebra II (Honors), Chemistry (Honors), Spanish III (Honors)
- Twelfth Grade: English IV (AP), Government (AP) / Economics (Honors), Pre-Calculus (Honors) or Calculus (Honors), Physics (Honors) or Biology II (Honors), Psychology.
- Electives: Marine Biology, Forensic Science, Psychology, Sociology, Speech, Computer, Web Design, Business, Yearbook, and Art I, II, and III

Special Needs

ASA is a school designed for "students who have distinct educational needs." The school states that it sets very defined goals but allows exceptional latitude for reaching those goals.

Foreign Languages

ASA offers instruction in Spanish.

Arts
ASA offers three art classes, Art I, II, and III.

Technology
Alexander Smith Academy does offer a computer course.

Extracurricular Activities
Because the school day is primarily just four days, Monday – Thursday, students are encouraged to participate in extra-curricular activities especially on Friday. The school does have some sponsored activities such as Student Council, Volunteer Service Club, and the literary magazine. It also hosts a National Honor Society chapter called Alpha Sigma Alpha.

Athletics
No information provided.

Alexander Smith Academy Fast Facts

Overview

School Type	Independent, Coeducational
Religious Affiliation	Nonsectarian
Date Founded	1968
Endowment	N/A
Grades Served	9-12
Enrollment	50
Grade 12	18
Grade 11	15
Grade 10	11
Grade 9	6
Student to Teacher Ratio	4:1
Faculty with Advanced Degrees (# / %)	N/A
Minorities in Student Body	14%

Curriculum

Academic Tracks Offered	On Track, Honors, AP
Advanced Placement Classes	4
Languages Offered	Spanish
Calendar (Semester / Trimester / Other)	N/A
Interscholastic Sports Programs	N/A

Graduating Seniors

National Merit Semi-Finalists (# / %)	0
Average SAT Scores (Class of 2010)	N/A
Mathematics	N/A
Critical Reading	N/A
Writing	N/A
% Students Admitted to 4 Year University	N/A

Admissions

Prime Entry Points	9
Tuition Grades 9-12	$26,600
Students on Financial Aid	Not Offered

Annunciation Orthodox School

3600 Yoakum Blvd., Houston, TX 77006
713-470-5600
www.AOSHouston.org

Mr. Mark Kelly, Head of School
Ms. Maria Newton, Director of Admissions

Overview

Annunciation Orthodox School (AOS) was established in the educational building of Annunciation Greek Orthodox Cathedral for early childhood children in 1970. AOS now serves Delphi Class (age 3) through the Eighth Grade, with a student body averaging 670 students. AOS provides a curriculum guided by the Greek Orthodox faith, with an emphasis on family and community. AOS received its accreditation through the Independent Schools Association of the Southwest in 1989.

Religious Affiliation

Annunciation Orthodox School bases its program on the Greek Orthodox Christian faith. AOS incorporates this faith's 2,000-year-old traditions and history into its curriculum through weekly religion courses and chapel services. Middle school students are required to attend AGAPE and participate in the Chapel Buddy Program. AGAPE is an assembly held each week on Monday, Tuesday, and Friday and includes 5-minute speeches given by seventh and eighth grade students (every student must give one speech each year). The Chapel Buddy Program pairs a seventh grader with a kindergartener in an interactive relationship that extends into eighth grade. They attend chapel and participate in a number of activities together. AOS respects diverse cultures and religious backgrounds in its students and faculty and encourages its students to do the same.

Location and Facilities

The school is located near the corner of Montrose and West Alabama, just across from St. Thomas University. AOS's campus features a running track, athletic field, activity center, and a 64,000 square foot building all of which cover two city blocks. The neighborhood surrounding the campus of AOS includes the Menil Collection and the Rothko Chapel.

Admissions

The application process includes 1) the online application; 2) a student photo; 3) a copy of the student's transcript (grades 1-8); 4) teacher recommendation forms; 5) standardized test scores; and 6) a group assessment/test. Students entering the Delphi Class (age 3), Prekindergarten (age 4), and Kindergarten (age 5) must be of age by July 15th, while students entering first grade must be 6 years of age by September 1st and have completed a year in a full-day kindergarten program. A professional diagnostician administers the WISC for grades one through four, while students in Kindergarten are given the WPPSI.

With the exception of the Delphi Class and Preschool students, all applicants must have Teacher Recommendation Forms completed and sent to the school by the student's current teacher. Students entering grades five through eight must complete either the WISC or OLSAT and complete the ISEE on campus or at an approved ISEE testing site. Students entering grades five through eight must also be interviewed by AOS and visit the school for half a day with a shadow host.

Academic Tracks and Curriculum

AOS provides an advanced academic track and Pre-AP courses that are designed to be intensive and challenging. The Lower School develops students' capabilities in art, creative writing, computer skills, Greek (language and history), social studies, language arts, religion, math, and study skills. The Middle School further challenges students in these same subjects, while introducing Spanish, science, digital photography, and drama. On-Track courses are not offered at AOS, only Honors and Pre-AP courses.

Special Needs
No information provided.

Foreign Languages
Annunciation Orthodox School instructs students in pre-school to fourth grade in Greek and students in sixth to eighth grade in Spanish. Both languages are required. AOS introduces students to foreign languages through the culture and history of ancient Greece and Hispanic peoples. Students interact with the breadth of Greek mythology and learn the stories of the Greek Pantheon. In Spanish, students study the influence of Hispanic culture in North and South America.

Arts
AOS incorporates enrichment courses into its curriculum that allow students to explore self-expression through art, digital photography, music, and drama. Students demonstrate their artistic talents at the end of each academic year in AOS's Night of the Arts celebration. Art projects are put on display for the AOS community to view, and students demonstrate their musical abilities in performances.

Technology
As part of the curriculum, students at AOS are introduced to computers as early as Pre-School. Students are instructed in the uses of Word, Excel, PowerPoint, online research, computer languages, HTML, and more. By the end of their eighth grade year, AOS students will have worked with CSS, WYSIWYG, and WIX.COM and will be proficient in the use of the QWERTY keyboard.

Extracurricular Activities
In music, students can participate in the Lower or Middle School Chorus, Chamber Choir, and the Orffestra (a small percussion group of Orff instruments). In drama, students can participate in plays, such as the 2011 performance of Meredith Willson's, "The Music Man." AOS publishes its own student led literary magazine called *Caught in the Pages*, which features art and writing from students (grades 2-8), faculty, and award winning pieces. AOS also highlights the importance of community service and provides students with access to numerous programs.

Athletics
AOS features five sports programs for boys, six for girls, and two co-ed programs. Boys and girls can participate in Track & Field (spring) and Cross Country (fall). Girls can participate in Field Hockey and Volleyball in the fall, Basketball and Soccer in the winter, and Lacrosse and Softball in the spring. Boys can participate in Football and Volleyball in the fall, Basketball and Soccer in the winter, and Lacrosse in the spring. Track & Field and Cross Country are introduced in sixth grade, while all other sports programs are introduced in seventh grade.

Annunciation Orthodox School Fast Facts

Overview

School Type	Religious, Coeducational
Religious Affiliation	Greek Orthodox
Date Founded	1970
Endowment	N/A
Grades Served	Age 3 – 8th grade
Enrollment	678
Grade 8	73
Grade 7	71
Grade 6	74
Grade 5	77
Grade 4	60
Grade 3	62
Grade 2	60
Grade 1	60
Kindergarten	62
Pre-Kindergarten	79
Student to Teacher Ratio	11:1
Faculty with Advanced Degrees (# / %)	70/45%
Minorities in Student Body	15%

Curriculum

Academic Tracks Offered	Honors, Pre-AP
Languages Offered	Greek, Spanish
Calendar (Semester / Trimester / Other)	Semester
Interscholastic Sports Programs	9

Admissions

Natural Entry Points	Pre-K, K, 6
Open House/Tours	Appointment
Early Childhood: 5 half days	$13,600
Early Childhood: 5 full days	$15,500
Lower School: K - 4	$16,090
Upper School: 5 - 8	$18,135
New/Returning Student Fee	$500
8th Grade DC Trip	$1,335
Books and Supplies (Grade 5 – 8)	~$600
New Family Fee	$300
Students on Financial Aid	20%

The Awty International School

7455 Awty School Ln, Houston, TX 77055   Dr. Stephen Codrington, Head of School
713-686-4850   Ms. Erika Benavente, Director of Admissions
www.Awty.org

Overview

The Awty International School was originally founded as the Awty School in 1956 as a preschool, eventually adding an Upper School by 1975. In 1984, the Awty School merged with the French School of Houston and became the Awty International School, which is now the second largest international school in the United States. AIS is accredited by the Independent Schools Association of the Southwest, the Council of International Schools, and the French Ministry of Education.

Religious Affiliation

Awty does not have any religious affiliation.

Location and Facilities

The Awty International School's campus covers 15-acres of land and includes two covered basketball/volleyball courts, an athletics center, two soccer fields, and three gymnasiums. AIS is located just outside the 610 Loop, off of I-10 and Post Oak, in an urban area of professional offices and shopping centers. The campus is gated, with a security checkpoint at the entrance.

Admissions

AIS features two academic programs in which students can enroll: the International Section and the French Section. Depending on grade, students will need specific teacher recommendation forms and will need to take the WISC IV, WPPSI, or the OLSAT. Students entering Pre-K through 5th grade will need a Parent Statement, while students entering 6th grade to 12th grade will need a Student Statement, both of which provide the school a brief introduction to the student. Students entering grades 5 through 12 must take the ISEE.

Academic Tracks and Curriculum

Awty features two possible academic tracks that students may take. The French Section follows the requirements and curriculum as determined by the French Ministry. The French Section's curriculum is no different from any other international French accredited school and students earn a French Baccalauréat based upon their 11th and 12th grade test scores.

The International Section follows a very similar curriculum as those used in American schools up until the 10th grade. During the students' 11th and 12th grade years in the International Section, the curriculum follows the required path towards an International Baccalaureate diploma. In order to graduate, students are required to complete six subjects, three "Higher Level" and three "Standard Level" courses. These subjects include: first language, second language, math, science, social science, and an IB elective. Students must also complete 150 hours of CAS (community, action, and service), a 4,000-word research essay, and a capstone course titled "Theory of Knowledge."

Special Needs

No information provided.

Foreign Languages

Awty's student body is made up of children from more than 50 countries, and Awty's foreign language curriculum represents that diversity. Awty emphasizes fluency, and all language programs are structured with this emphasis in mind. Early Childhood students are enrolled in a dual-language program, where one day is in English and the other is in either French or Spanish. Middle School and Upper School language programs include Arabic, Chinese, Japanese, Dutch, French, German, Italian, Spanish, Portuguese, and Norwegian.

Arts

Awty integrates the fine arts into its curriculum as a demonstration that students who participate in the fine arts are more well rounded individuals. In the visual arts, students are exposed to many different types of media throughout their entire education, such as digital studio and photography. In the performing arts, 6th and 7th grade students participate in either the Triple Switch program, a set of six classes lasting one term each that includes music and theatre arts, or Band. Students in higher grades can participate in Awty's Choir, Orchestra, Dance ensembles, IB Art and Theatre courses, Jazz Band, and more.

Technology

No information provided.

Extracurricular Activities

As part of the requirements for the IB program, students attending Awty must earn CAS hours (Creativity, Action, and Service). Students may earn these hours through a number of extracurricular programs, including community service projects. Students may participate in a variety of clubs, such as language clubs, the Book Club, Anime Club, Guitar, Knitting, and Culinary Club. Awty also hosts a Literary Magazine, a Speech and Debate team, a Model United Nations, and much more.

Athletics

Students in grades 6 through 12 may participate in any of the sports programs available at the Awty International School. Middle School students play in the Greater Houston Athletic Conference and Upper School students play in The Texas Association of Private and Parochial Schools (TAPPS). Awty hosts Cross Country, Volleyball, Soccer, Basketball, Golf, Swimming, Track, and Tennis. Students may fulfill a portion of their CAS hours requirements by participating in sports.

Awty International School Fast Facts

Overview

School Type	International, Coeducational
Religious Affiliation	None
Date Founded	1956
Endowment (2011)	$4 million
Grades Served	Pre-K - 12
Enrollment	1206
Grade 12	84
Grade 11	85
Grade 10	96
Grade 9	88
Grade 8	84
Grade 7	81
Grade 6	94
Grade 5	86
Grade 4	76
Grade 3	82
Grade 2	88
Grade 1	80
Kindergarten	79
Pre-Kindergarten	103
Student to Teacher Ratio	7:1
Faculty with Advanced Degrees (# / %)	98 / 52%
Minorities in Student Body	26%

Curriculum

Academic Tracks Offered	French Section, IB Section
International Baccalaureate Courses	52
Languages Offered	IB Languages
Calendar (Semester / Trimester / Other)	Trimester
Interscholastic Sports Programs	8

Graduating Seniors

National Merit Semi-Finalists '12 (# / %)	1 / 1%
Average SAT Scores (Class of 2011)	1960
Mathematics	670
Critical Reading	630
Writing	660
% Students Admitted to 4 Year University	N/A

Admissions

Natural Entry Points	Pre-K, K, 6, 9
Preschool	$14,948
Kindergarten	$15,937
Lower School	$16,793
Middle School	$18,846
Grades 9-12	$20,472
Capital Building Fee	$1,000
Books and Supplies	~$600
New Family Fee	$800
IB Fee	$765
Students on Financial Aid	N/A

Bellaire High School

5100 Maple St., Bellaire, TX 77401
713-667-2064
www.Bellaire.org

Mr. Tim Salem, Principal
Ms. Rosalon Moorhead, Magnet Coordinator

Overview

Bellaire High School started in 1955 and was the first International Baccalaureate (IB) School in Texas. With its IB program and its World Languages magnet program, Bellaire focuses on international relations. Bellaire's goal is to create "...active learners, well-rounded individuals, and engaged citizens, who gain the practical experience of being part of an international community." The city of Bellaire and parts of Houston, such as Meyerland and Braesmont, are zoned to Bellaire High School.

Religious Affiliation

As a public school, Bellaire has no religious affiliation. According to Houston Independent School District's policy, every school has a moment of silence each day during which students can pray silently to themselves if they so choose. Also, absences because of religious holidays do not count toward the student's total number of absences. However, the student is still responsible for the makeup work.

Location and Facilities

Bellaire High School sits on the corner of S. Rice Ave. and Maple St in Bellaire. The original building is three stories, and Bellaire recently added a new, three-story science wing with more classrooms and science labs. The school's approximately 7-acre lot further includes a traditional theatre and a library as well as a dance room, an orchestra room, a band room, and a choir room.

Admissions

Bellaire's admissions process is split into two different types: zoned and magnet.

For students zoned to Bellaire, as long as they attended an HISD middle school that feeds into Bellaire, Bellaire will receive their information automatically from the middle school. If the student did not attend an HISD middle school that feeds into Bellaire, then Bellaire needs the parent and student to register over the summer. The parent must bring in the following information: 1) Student's Birth Certificate or Passport, 2) Previous Year's Final Report Card, 3) Copy of Transcript/Permanent Record, 4) Student's Social Security card (if they have one), 5) Copy of Immunization Record, and 6) Proof of HISD Residency in Bellaire's zone. Note that students zoned to Bellaire who wish to participate in the magnet program are automatically accepted into the program. The student does not need to fill out an application or take the test.

For the World Languages Magnet Program, all students must take the Modern Language Aptitude Test, fill out the application, and submit the following information: 1) Most Recent Report Card, 2) Previous Year's Final Report Card, 3) Copy of Transcript/Permanent Record, 4) Two Years of Standardized Test Scores, 5) Copy of Immunization Record, and 6) Proof of HISD Residency.

Bellaire offers testing during the second or third week of January. Every applicant has to take the test. Bellaire asks that the students arrive 30 minutes before the test is scheduled and that they bring two #2 pencils and photo identification.

Academic Tracks and Curriculum

Bellaire offers three tracks—On Track, IB, and AP. Pre-AP classes lead to the 22 classes from the College Board's Advanced Placement (AP) curriculum. Bellaire's AP courses include: AP English Language, AP English Literature, AP Art History, AP Biology, AP Environmental Science, AP Chemistry, AP Computer Science A/AB, AP

U.S. History, AP Government U.S./Comparative, AP Human Geography, AP Economics Macro/Micro, AP European History, AP Art 2D, AP Art Drawing, AP Chinese Language, AP French Language, AP French Literature, AP German Language, and AP Italian Language.

In order to graduate with an IB Diploma, students are required to complete six subjects—three Higher Level and three Standard Level courses. These subjects include: first language, second language, math, science, social science, and an IB elective. Students must also complete 150 hours of CAS (community, action, and service), a 4,000-word research essay, and a capstone course titled Theory of Knowledge.

In order to graduate with a Recommended Diploma, students must complete 26 credits; one credit equals one year of study: English (4), Social Studies (4), Math (4), Science (4), Foreign Language (2), Physical Education (1), Speech (1/2), Fine Art (1), and Electives (5 and 1/2). A Distinguished Diploma requires one more year of a foreign language and one less year of an elective.

Special Needs
Standard HISD procedures.

Foreign Languages
With its World Languages Magnet Program, Bellaire offers courses in eleven languages: Arabic, French, German, Hebrew, Hindi, Italian, Japanese, Latin, Russian, Spanish, and Mandarin. Non-magnet students must complete at least two years of a foreign language to graduate—three years if the student wishes to earn a Distinguished Diploma. Magnet students must take four years of one language and one year of a second language, or if they completed one year of their first language in middle school, they can take three years of the first language and two of the second language.

Arts
Bellaire students must complete at least one year of a fine art elective to graduate. The options include band, dance team, dance classes, orchestra, choir, and theatre arts. UIL sponsors all but the dance classes, so all other options participate in competitions against other schools through the University Interscholastic League.

Technology
In its multiple computer labs, Bellaire offers AP Computer Science A and AB, IB Computer Science, Web Technologies, and Digital and Interactive Media as a part of its career and technical education department. However, a technology credit is no longer required to graduate.

Extracurricular Activities
Bellaire offers a number of different clubs and activities to its students. Some examples include: Astronomy Club, Culinary Club, Jazz Club, Model United Nations, Mock Trial, National Honor Society, Quidditch Club, and Yoga Club. UIL activities include: yearbook, theatre, cheerleading, debate, guitar, and newspaper.

Athletics
Bellaire has twelve UIL sports teams, including: football, baseball, softball, volleyball, and boys' and girls' basketball, wrestling, soccer, track, cross-country, tennis, golf, and swimming. Also, Bellaire includes one non-UIL sport, boys' and girls' lacrosse. Athletic facilities include a gym, a baseball field and an outdoor track.

Bellaire High School Fast Facts

Overview

School Type	Public, Magnet, Coeducational
Religious Affiliation	None
Date Founded	1955
Grades Served	9-12
Enrollment	3377
Grade 12	706
Grade 11	785
Grade 10	938
Grade 9	948
Student to Teacher Ratio	18:1
Faculty with Advanced Degrees (#/%)	45/23 %
Minorities in Student Body	67 %

Curriculum

Academic Tracks Offered	On Track, IB, AP
Advanced Placement Courses Offered	22
Languages Offered	IB including Arabic, French, German, Hebrew, Hindi, Italian, Japanese, Latin, Russian, Spanish, and Mandarin
Calendar (Semester / Trimester / Other)	Semester
Interscholastic Sports Programs	12

Graduating Seniors

National Merit Semi-Finalists (#/%)	38/ 5 %
Average SAT Scores (Class of 2012)	1682
Mathematics	583
Critical Reading	548
Writing	551
% Students Admitted to 4 Year University	N/A

Public School Stats

Gifted and Talented Students	24%
Free & Reduced Lunch	40%
AYP (2006-2010)	Met AYP
AYP (2010-2011)	Missed AYP
TEA Accountability (2006-2008)	Academically Acceptable
TEA Accountability (2008-2010)	Recognized
TEA Accountability (2010-2013)	Academically Acceptable

Robert M. Beren Academy

11333 Cliffwood, Houston, TX 77035   Rabbi Harry Sinoff, Head of School
713-723-7170   Ms. Samantha Steinberg, Director of Admissions
www.BerenAcademy.org

Overview

Robert M. Beren Academy was originally founded in 1969 as The South Texas Hebrew Academy at the corner of South Braeswood and Chimney Rock. In 1998, the Israel Henry Beren Foundation donated to the school and the school's name was changed in appreciation to Robert M. Beren Academy, or RMBA. RMBA is affiliated with the Yeshiva University and the Association of Modern Orthodox Day Schools and is the only Jewish day school in Houston to serve students in preschool to 12th grade.

Religious Affiliation

RMBA is a private, Modern Orthodox Jewish school that strongly emphasizes the incorporation of Judaic studies with a college preparatory curriculum. All students take part in studying Chumash, Navi, Mishna, Gemara, Jewish Philosophy, and Halacha throughout the entirety of the curriculum.

Location and Facilities

RMBA moved to its 54,000 square foot campus at Cliffwood in 1999, which resides on 52 acres of land. The campus includes a 10,000 square foot library, multiple laboratories, a gymnasium, an art room, and athletic fields.

Admissions

All prospective students must complete the online application form and submit medical, teacher recommendation, and records release forms. Students must also submit their standardized test scores and any evaluation forms. According to the Head of School, Rabbi Ari Segal, RMBA admits observant Jewish students as well as non-observant in order to diversify the religious community and demonstrate that the Torah is for all to study.

Academic Tracks and Curriculum

RMBA features a dual-curriculum of Judaic studies and secular studies. From grades 1 to 5, students may choose to participate in the traditional educational track or the Montessori track. The curriculum for grades 6 through 8 follows the traditional track, regardless of the student. Students in grades 9 through 12 will follow either the normal track or the AP track.

A student must earn 33 credits and annually complete 25 hours of community service to graduate; one credit equals one year of study: English (4), Math (3), Science (3), Social Studies (4), Foreign Language (3), Physical Education (1), Electives (3), and Judaic Studies (12). Two semesters equals one credit.

Special Needs

The school employs three counselors who provide regular assistance to students with diagnosed learning differences.

Foreign Languages

As part of the school's Judaic Studies, students must complete up to Advanced Hebrew in their Foreign Language requirement. No other foreign languages are offered at RMBA.

Arts

Students attending RMBA are required to complete one course in the Fine Arts. Students will have the choice to either take Art, such as Graphic Design and Studio Art, or Drama.

Technology

RMBA supplies students with a computer lab that has twenty-two workstations. Faculty utilizes Smart Boards in the classroom and interacts with students and parents via Edline, an online educational tool where teachers may post assignments, grades, and send emails to parents.

Extracurricular Activities

RMBA hosts a number of programs for students to interact with one another throughout the school year. Students may join the Math and Science Club, the National Honor Society, the Yearbook staff, and Student Government and participate in many community service opportunities. During the summer, students ranging from 18 months to sixth grade may apply to attend Camp Moshava Houston, which is broken up into Machaneh Aleph (18 months to Kindergarten) and Machaneh Bet (grades 1 to 6).

Athletics

RMBA features four interscholastic sports programs (Volleyball, Golf, Basketball, and Soccer) and two intramural sports programs (Football and Softball). Beren competes in the Texas Association of Private and Parochial Schools (TAPPS).

Beren Academy Fast Facts

Overview

School Type	Religious, Coeducational
Religious Affiliation	Modern Orthodox Jewish
Date Founded	1969
Endowment	N/A
Grades Served	Preschool-12th
Enrollment	284

Grade 12	19	Grade 6	20
Grade 11	13	Grade 5	18
Grade 10	20	Grade 4	21
Grade 9	13	Grade 3	34
Grade 8	14	Grade 2	18
Grade 7	19	Grade 1	33
Kindergarten			8
Pre-Kindergarten			34

Student to Teacher Ratio	7:1
Faculty with Advanced Degrees (# / %)	17/71%
Minorities in Student Body	5%

Curriculum

Academic Tracks Offered	On Track, AP, Montessori
Advanced Placement Courses Offered	12
Languages Offered	Hebrew
Calendar (Semester / Trimester / Other)	Semester
Interscholastic Sports Programs	4

Graduating Seniors

National Merit Semi-Finalists '11 (# / %)	0
Average SAT Scores (Class of 2010)	1873
Mathematics	628
Critical Reading	642
Writing	603
% Students Admitted to 4 Year University	N/A

Admissions

Prime Entry Points	Preschool, 1, 6, 9
Pre-K	$6,662-$8,363
Kindergarten	$10,790
Grades 1-4	$14,539
Grade 5	$14,971
Grade 6	$16,120
Grades 7-8	$16,281
Grade 9	$18,070
Grades 10-12	$18,883
Tuition Deposit	$500
New Student Fee	$100
Students on Financial Aid	N/A

Briarwood School

11207 Whittington Dr., Houston, TX 77077   Ms. Carole C. Wills, Head of School
281-493-1070   Ms. Priscilla Mitchell, Director of Admissions
www.BriarwoodSchool.org

Overview

In 1967, Yvonne and Dave Streit founded The Briarwood School after their search for an institution capable of educating their severely handicapped daughter proved futile. Ms. Streit sampled special needs programs across the country, including Purdue and UCLA, and compiled her own program based on the information she had researched. Ms. Streit enlisted the aid of a special education teacher, an art teacher, and a physical therapist and began instructing six students in her backyard. Briarwood School has since moved to west Houston and over 9,000 students have attended Briarwood School since its inception.

Religious Affiliation

The Briarwood School does not have any religious affiliation.

Location and Facilities

Briarwood School is located between Dairy Ashford, Westheimer, Kirkwood, and Briarforest Drive on 9.2 acres of land. The 80,000 square foot school building contains modern athletics facilities, nine computer labs, and a Media Center.

Admissions

Parents must complete the Enrollment Application and submit recent (within 2 years) testing information. The Briarwood School staff will review the submitted material, conduct an assessment session with the student, and interview the parent. After the assessment session, if the school's enrollment status permits, the student will be offered the opportunity to enroll with Briarwood School.

Testing information includes an intelligence test (WISC IV or WJ III NU Test of Cognitive Abilities), academic testing (Woodcock-Johnson or Wechsler Individual Achievement Test), and the student's current school's achievement tests. The Enrollment Application requires parents to submit information regarding their student's developmental history, therapy and counseling history, and all educational evaluations. The Briarwood School will not contact the parent for an interview until all information is sent to the school by the mentioned professionals on the Enrollment Application.

Academic Tracks and Curriculum

Briarwood School prides itself on its ability to create prescriptive curriculum for each student's needs. The Lower School features classrooms of 8-10 students (according to age, socialization, and academic abilities) that are self-contained. The Middle and Upper Schools also include students diagnosed with learning differences and emphasize self-advocacy in order to ensure that the student's needs are being met. The Tuttle School is designed for students, age 5 to 21, who are developmentally delayed. The classrooms are capped at 8 students with a teacher and teacher's aide at the helm. The Tuttle School emphasizes motor and living skills and provides students with pre-vocational and vocational experiences.

Special Needs

Briarwood School's focus since its founding has been the support of students with average to superior intelligence who are not necessarily accommodated by the traditional classroom setting, as well as supporting students who are developmentally delayed. Briarwood School's curriculum and programs are designed to cater to each student's personal educational needs.

Foreign Languages
The school does not offer any foreign languages.

Arts
As part of Briarwood School's curriculum, students are offered the chance to participate in the theatre arts as an elective. The Middle and Upper Schools feature a Drama Class, which focuses on developing the students' acting abilities. Students in the Upper School are also given the opportunity to join the Company Class, a course that exposes students to all aspects of theatre arts production.

Technology
Briarwood School's facilities and classrooms include 170 computers, which are a mixture of PC and MAC platforms. Briarwood School utilizes special education software packages in order to help individualize each student's instruction and determine the student's progress, such as CornerStone, SkillsBank, and Essential Learning Systems (ELS).

Extracurricular Activities
Students attending the Briarwood School are given the option to participate in a number of electives and activities as part of the curriculum. Students may join the student council, prepare for the job market in a business skills course, and/or design the school's yearbook.

Athletics
Students attending the Tuttle School are given the opportunity to participate in the Special Olympics Texas (SOTX) as early as age 8. To compete on the state level, students must be at least 12 years of age. Students in grades 7 through 12 are eligible to participate in the school's interscholastic sports program. The school fields teams in eight sports: Basketball, Cross Country, Golf, Soccer, Tennis, Track, Volleyball, and Winter Sports. The school is a member of the Texas Association of Private and Parochial Schools.

Briarwood School Fast Facts

Overview

School Type	Special Needs, Coeducational
Religious Affiliation	None
Date Founded	1967
Endowment	N/A
Grades Served	K-12
Enrollment	458
Grade 12	45
Grade 11	31
Grade 10	20
Grade 9	24
Grade 8	26
Grade 7	34
Grade 6	21
Grade 5	35
Grade 4	31
Grade 3	23
Grade 2	12
Grade 1	8
Tuttle School (age 5-21)	145
Student to Teacher Ratio	7:1
Faculty with Advanced Degrees (# / %)	N/A
Minorities in Student Body	12%

Curriculum

Academic Tracks Offered	On Track, Learning Differences, Delayed Development
Advanced Placement Courses Offered	None
Languages Offered	None
Calendar (Semester / Trimester / Other)	Semester
Interscholastic Sports Programs	8

Graduating Seniors

National Merit Semi-Finalists (# / %)	None
Average SAT Scores (Class of 2010)	N/A
Mathematics	N/A
Critical Reading	N/A
Writing	N/A
% Students Admitted to 4 Year University	85%

Admissions

Prime Entry Points	K, 1, 7, 9
Lower School (K-6)	$17,100
Middle School (7-8)	$17,250
Upper School (9-12)	$17,250
Returning Student Fee	$225-$350
New Student Fee	$650
Books and Supplies	$120-400
Activity Fee	$50-$400
Students on Financial Aid	N/A

British School of Houston

4211 Watonga Blvd., Houston, TX 77092   Mr. Stephen Foxwell, Head of School
713-290-9025   Ms. Tami Riggs, Director of Admissions
www.BritishSchoolOfHouston.org

Overview

The British School of Houston is part of World Class Learning Schools, a division of the for-profit company World Class Learning Group. BSH has developed an academic program based on the International Primary Curriculum, the National Curriculum for England and Wales, and the International Baccalaureate Diploma Program.

All of BSH's teachers are required to have teaching degrees from the United Kingdom. Students are introduced to both British English and American English at an early age utilizing educational material from America and Britain. The school is open to children of all nationalities. Approximately 60% of the student body is British, 7% American, and the remaining 33% come from countries such as The Netherlands, Oman, Australia, Singapore, and Egypt.

Religious Affiliation

The British School does not have any religious affiliation.

Location and Facilities

The British School of Houston's campus is located on 14 acres of land near the 610 Loop and I-290. It is bordered on the north by single-family homes, on the northeast by two churches, on the south and east by multi-family dwellings, and on the west by railroad tracks.

Admissions

BSH features an open enrollment policy, in which students may apply throughout the year and are admitted based upon openings in enrollment. However, students generally begin at the start of the academic year. Siblings of currently enrolled students are given priority but are not guaranteed enrollment. The admissions office also takes into consideration an even balance of the sexes within the classrooms, thus the minority sex may receive priority.

The admissions process consists of three steps: 1) Application 2) Assessment Visit and 3) Enrollment. The Application is composed of a) application and essay b) application fee c) school transcripts and d) teacher evaluations – Math and English for 6-12th grade. Following the receipt of the application, students are invited to meet with a member of the assessment team. If the school deems the application and assessment visit adequate, an offer of enrollment is made so long as space is available.

Academic Tracks and Curriculum

Students in the Early Years (ages 3 to 5) follow the Foundation Curriculum with a focus on six areas of education, such as social development and mathematical development. Students enrolled in the Primary School (ages 5 to 11) are instructed using the International Primary Curriculum and the National Curriculum of England, which includes a three to six week period of study on real-life interests. Middle School students (ages 11 to 14) follow the National Curriculum which structures twelve disciplines into a circular method of education. High School students continue to follow the National Curriculum by way of the International General Certificates of Secondary Education examinations, which act as a preparatory tool for the International Baccalaureate Diploma Program. In their final two years, students follow the curriculum designed by the IBDP, which includes CAS (Creativity, Action, and Service) hours.

In order to graduate, students are required to complete six subjects, three Higher Level and three Standard Level courses. These subjects include: first language, second language, math, science, social science, and an IB elective. Students must also complete 150 hours of CAS, a 4,000-word research essay, and a capstone course titled Theory of Knowledge.

Special Needs

No information provided about accommodations for students with learning differences such as ADHD, dysgraphia, or processing disorders. However, the British School of Houston prides itself on its differentiated instruction: "BSH teachers tailor their instruction and adjust the curriculum to students' needs rather than expecting students to modify themselves for the curriculum."

Foreign Languages

Students attending BSH may study French and Spanish.

Arts

BSH considers the fine arts an important part of the student's education experience. BSH offers students the opportunity to participate in a number of musicals and dramas, school choirs, ballet, recorder and trumpet ensembles, and more. Performances are held throughout the academic year. As part of the curriculum, students are introduced to digital design and design technology.

Music receives special attention at BSH. Housed in a new building built in 2009, the Music Department has access to three teaching rooms and a large practice room where approximately 80 instrumental lessons take place per week. Music instruction begins at the Foundation level and, beginning with Year 5, the school encourages students to form their own bands. Major music performances include three winter concerts, an annual piano recital, and a rock concert.

Technology

No information provided.

Extracurricular Activities

BSH assigns each enrolling student to one of four Houses: Air, Earth, Wind, and Fire. Throughout the year, students are awarded House Points based on outstanding performance in all aspects of their education. Individually, House Points will earn students certificates, such as the Platinum House Certificate (150 points), while students also earn their assigned House points from House events. Students may participate in several Academic clubs (such as IB Chemistry Revision), the school newspaper (Students Extra!), and various opportunities for community service.

Athletics

BSH hosts seven sports programs in which students may participate, including several athletics clubs. The current sports programs are Rugby, Track & Field, Touch Rugby, Soccer, Netball, Golf, and Volleyball. The school's mascot is the Bulldog and the sports teams have participated in the Texas Association of Private and Parochial Schools, Texas Youth Rugby Association, and Florida Netball Classic.

British School Fast Facts

Overview

School Type	International, Coeducational
Religious Affiliation	Non-Sectarian
Date Founded	2000
Endowment	None
Grades Served	Nursery-13 Year (Preschool-12th)

Enrollment	521
Grade 12	21
Grade 11	24
Grade 10	45
Grade 9	25
Grade 8	51
Grade 7	47
Grade 6	48
Grade 5	46
Grade 4	45
Grade 3	29
Grade 2	29
Grade 1	38
Kindergarten	33
Pre-Kindergarten	40
Student to Teacher Ratio	7:1
Faculty with Advanced Degrees (#/%)	N/A
Minorities in Student Body	20%

Curriculum

Academic Tracks Offered	IB Diploma
International Baccalaureate Courses	N/A
Languages Offered	French, Spanish
Calendar (Semester / Trimester / Other)	Trimester
Interscholastic Sports Programs	7

Graduating Seniors

National Merit Semi-Finalists (#/%)	0
Average SAT Scores (Class of 2010)	N/A
Mathematics	N/A
Critical Reading	N/A
Writing	N/A
% Students Admitted to 4 Year University	N/A

Admissions

Prime Entry Points	All
Nursery (5 half days)	$10,360
Nursery (3 full days)	$12,430
Nursery (Full-time) to Year 6	$19,050
Senior School (Year 7 to 11)	$20,870
IB Program (Year 12 and 13)	$23,070
IB Testing Fee (Year 12 and 13)	$1,350
New Student Fee	$2,000
Enrollment Deposit (Refundable)	$1,000
Students on Financial Aid	None

Carnegie Vanguard High School

1501 Taft St., Houston, TX 77019
713-732-3690
www.CarnegieVanguard.com

Mr. Ramon Moss, Principal
Ms. Melaney Aschner, Magnet/GT Coordinator

Overview

Carnegie Vanguard High School (CVHS) started as a school-within-a-school Vanguard program at Jesse H. Jones Senior High School in 1977. In 2002, CVHS became an independent high school. CVHS's mission is "to provide a unique and challenging learning environment to prepare the diverse gifted & talented population of Houston Independent School District for leadership in a global society."

Religious Affiliation

As a public school, Carnegie Vanguard High School has no religious affiliation. According to Houston Independent School District's policy, every school has a moment of silence each day during which students can pray silently to themselves if they so choose. Also, absences because of religious holidays do not count toward the student's total number of absences. However, the student is still responsible for the makeup work.

Location and Facilities

Due to open in the fall of 2012, Carnegie is constructing a new campus on a 6-acre lot at the corner of West Gray and Taft next to Gregory Lincoln Magnet School. The school is being designed to be LEED certified with green facilities and operations, including a green roof. Many views from within the campus will face inward to two courtyards, which is designed to emulate a small liberal arts college. Carnegie's new campus intends to include a parking garage, tennis courts, gym, library, amphitheater, and a large open green for soccer, volleyball, and baseball. The historic Settegast building will house the school's Fine Arts program.

Admissions

Carnegie's admission process is split between applicants who are already identified as Gifted and Talented (G/T) in HISD and those who are not already identified at G/T. Both prospects must complete the Carnegie Vanguard Application (they do not accept the Magnet application) and demonstrate proof of HISD residency.

Students already identified as G/T in HISD must submit along with the application their HISD G/T Middle School Identification Matrix (or G/T profile sheet) and a copy of their G/T status report.

Students not already identified as G/T in HISD or attending a private school must submit along with the application their previous year's final report card and a Teacher Recommendation Form. If available, students must also submit their most recent Stanford/Aprenda results (within the last 12 months) and Naglieri (NNAT-2) results (current year). If a student currently attends an HISD school but is not considered G/T, then the student must complete the NNAT-2. If a student currently attends a private school, then the student must complete both the NNAT-2 and the Stanford test.

Qualified applications are then placed into a lottery if the number of applications outnumbers the number of available positions at Carnegie. The school reserves 20% of its openings for applicants whose siblings are currently enrolled and gives extra weight to students who are of low socio-economic status. A separate lottery is held should the number of legacy applicants exceed the number of reserved positions.

Academic Tracks and Curriculum

Carnegie Vanguard offers one track—AP. Pre-AP classes lead to the 20 classes from the College Board's Advanced Placement (AP) curriculum. The only Honors classes are electives. CVHS offers these AP courses: AP English Language, AP English Literature, AP Art History, AP Spanish Language, AP Spanish Literature, AP Calculus AB/BC, AP Statistics, AP Biology, AP Environmental Science, AP Physics, AP Chemistry, AP Computer Science, AP Human Geography, AP World History, AP U.S. History, AP Government, AP Economics Macro/Micro, and AP European History. Carnegie encourages its students to earn a Distinguished Diploma.

In order to graduate with a Recommended Diploma, students must complete 26 credits; one credit is equal to one year of study: English (4), Social Studies (4), Math (4), Science (4), Foreign Language (2), Physical Education (1), Speech (1/2), Fine Art (1), and Electives (5 and 1/2). A Distinguished Diploma requires one more year of a foreign language.

Special Needs

Standard HISD procedures.

Foreign Languages

CVHS students must complete at least three years of a foreign language to graduate. Instruction in several languages is offered—Latin up to Latin IV, Spanish up to Spanish III followed by AP Spanish Language and AP Spanish Literature, French up to French IV (Language and Culture AP), Mandarin, and Arabic (currently only counts an elective). If a student has completed a language credit in seventh and eighth grade, then one foreign language credit is earned towards graduation.

Arts

CVHS students must complete at least one year of a fine art elective to graduate. Some of the more notable options include art I-IV, theatre, and photography. Carnegie plans to repurpose the Settegast building to house its Fine Arts program. The building is intended to include a theatre, photography studio, art studio, and music studio with access to the outside amphitheater. Carnegie is also planning on repurposing a former Orange Crush facility into a performing arts building at a later date.

Technology

CVHS offers Business Information Management as a part of its career and technical education department and AP Computer Science as part of its science department, but a technology credit is no longer required to graduate.

Extracurricular Activities

CVHS offers a number of different clubs and activities to its students. Some examples include: UIL (University Interscholastic League) Academic Competitions, Photography Club, Checkers Club, Model United Nations, Live Music Club, Yearbook, Newspaper, and National Honor Society.

Athletics

Students are not required to participate in a sport at CVHS. The school has only two UIL teams: baseball and volleyball. However, it does offer more sports through its clubs: cross country/track, soccer, and tennis. Carnegie intends to include four tennis courts, two baseball fields, a beach volleyball court, and a multi-purpose gymnasium with the new campus.

Carnegie Vanguard High School Fast Facts

Overview

School Type	Public, Magnet, Vanguard, Coeducational
Religious Affiliation	None
Date Founded	2002
Grades Served	9-12
Enrollment	524
9th Grade	197
10th Grade	124
11th Grade	119
12th Grade	84
Student to Teacher Ratio	16:1
Faculty with Advanced Degrees (# / %)	7/31 %
Minorities in Student Body	56 %

Curriculum

Academic Tracks Offered	AP
Advanced Placement Courses Offered	20
Languages Offered	Arabic, Chinese, French, Latin, and Spanish
Calendar (Semester / Trimester / Other)	Semester
Interscholastic Sports Programs	2

Graduating Seniors

National Merit Semi-Finalists (# / %)	2/ 2.5 %
Average SAT Scores (Class of 2012)	1849
Mathematics	624
Critical Reading	613
Writing	612
% Students Admitted to 4 Year University	90-95%

Public School Stats

Gifted and Talented Students	98%
Free & Reduced Lunch	28%
AYP (2006-2011)	Met AYP
TEA Accountability (2006-2013)	Exemplary

Michael E. DeBakey High School for Health Professions

3100 Shenandoah St., Houston, TX 77021   Ms. Agnes Bell, Principal
713-741-2410   D. Rios, Magnet Coordinator
schools.houstonisd.org/DeBakey

Overview

In 1972, DeBakey opened at Baylor College of Medicine. Now on its own campus, DeBakey keeps close ties to the Texas Medical Center, giving students the opportunity to experience the Medical Center's healthcare and research facilities while still in high school. DeBakey's mission is "to provide a challenging, well-balanced college preparatory program which focuses on educational experiences in science and the health professions and to further an understanding of [a] multicultural community."

Religious Affiliation

As a public school, DeBakey has no religious affiliation. According to Houston Independent School District's policy, every school has a moment of silence each day during which students can pray silently to themselves if they so choose. Also, absences because of religious holidays do not count toward the student's total number of absences. However, the student is still responsible for the makeup work.

Location and Facilities

Currently residing east of the Medical Center, DeBakey is at 3100 Shenandoah St. near 288. Originally, DeBakey resided in Baylor College of Medicine and was named The High School for Health Professions. In 1996, the school was renamed to honor the famous cardiac surgeon, Michael DeBakey. The campus features a three-story building with twenty rooms per floor. The campus also includes a library, auditorium, and separate testing rooms.

Admissions

The DeBakey admissions process includes an application and a test. All students must fill out the application and submit with it the following information: 1) Most Recent Report Card, 2) Previous Year's Final Report Card, 3) Test Record Card and 4) Proof of HISD Residency.

Once the application is completed and submitted, the parent needs to schedule an admissions test with the Magnet Office (713-746-5205). Every applicant has to take the test. DeBakey asks that the students arrive 30 minutes before the test is scheduled and that they bring two #2 pencils and photo identification.

Academic Tracks and Curriculum

DeBakey offers two tracks—On Track and AP. Pre-AP classes lead to the 15 classes from the College Board's Advanced Placement (AP) curriculum. DeBakey offers these AP courses: AP Biology, AP Chemistry, AP Physics, AP Calculus AB/BC, AP Statistics, AP English Language, AP English Literature, AP Economics, AP World History, AP U.S. History, AP Government, AP Spanish Language, and AP French Language.

DeBakey only offers a more rigorous **Distinguished Diploma**, which requires more credits to graduate. Students must complete 32 credits: English (4), Social Studies (4), Math (5), Science (5), Foreign Language (3), Athletics (1), Health (.5), Speech (.5), Fine Art (1), SAT Prep (.5), Study Skills (.5), Information Systems (1), and Health Science (4). Students must also complete 100 hours of community service.

Special Needs

Standard HISD procedures.

Foreign Languages

DeBakey's "Language Other Than English Department" bases their program around a five-part objective, called the "Five C's." These objectives are Communication, Cultures, Connections, Comparisons, and Communities. DeBakey students must complete three years of a foreign language to graduate. Instruction in two languages is offered—French and Spanish up to AP Language.

Arts

DeBakey students must complete at least one year of a fine art elective to graduate. The options include art I-II and theatre productions.

Technology

DeBakey has four computer labs with approximately twenty to twenty-five computers in each one. DeBakey offers Business Communication Information Systems and Web Mastering as a part of its career and technical education department.

Extracurricular Activities

DeBakey offers a number of different clubs and activities to its students. Some examples include: Debate, Yearbook, Student Council, Newspaper, Ceramics/Sculpture, and Community Service.

Athletics

Since DeBakey's health science curriculum requires so much after school time, DeBakey does not have any official sports teams. However, students are allowed to participate at the school's sports program to which they are zoned. The student needs to contact DeBakey's Physical Education teachers or administration to determine what is required to participate in these school's sports programs.

DeBakey High School Fast Facts

Overview
School Type	Public, Magnet, Coeducational
Religious Affiliation	None
Date Founded	1972
Grades Served	9-12
Enrollment	887
Grade 12	189
Grade 11	227
Grade 10	216
Grade 9	255
Student to Teacher Ratio	16:1
Faculty with Advanced Degrees (# / %)	25/49 %
Minorities in Student Body	92 %

Curriculum
Academic Tracks Offered	On Track, AP
Advanced Placement Courses Offered	15
Languages Offered	Spanish, French
Calendar (Semester / Trimester / Other)	Semester
Interscholastic Sports Programs	0

Graduating Seniors
National Merit Semi-Finalists (# / %)	8/ 4%
Average SAT Scores (Class of 2012)	1808
Mathematics	645
Critical Reading	574
Writing	589
% Students Admitted to 4 Year University	N/A

Public School Stats
Gifted and Talented Students	55%
Free & Reduced Lunch	48%
AYP (2006-2011)	Met AYP
TEA Accountability (2006-2013)	Exemplary

Duchesne Academy of the Sacred Heart

10202 Memorial Dr., Houston, TX 77024   Ms. Jan Dunn, RSCJ, Headmistress
713-468-8211   Ms. Beth Speck, Director of Admissions
www.Duchesne.org

Overview

Duchesne Academy of the Sacred Heart was founded in 1960 as part of the Network of Sacred Heart Schools. The school derives its name from Saint Rose Philippine Duchesne, a Catholic nun, French saint, and founder of the first houses of the Society of the Sacred Heart in America. Duchesne is an all-girls school and began its enrollment in 1960 with 52 students in 7th, 8th, and 9th grades. Today, the school educates over 600 girls from Pre-kindergarten to the 12th grade. Duchesne is also a part of the Roman Catholic Archdiocese of Galveston-Houston.

Religious Affiliation

Duchesne is a Catholic, college preparatory school that incorporates the Catholic faith into its curriculum. The Society of the Sacred Heart was founded in 1800 in France by Saint Madeleine Sophie Barat and allows membership only to women. The Society emphasizes women's education, and Saint Rose Philippine Duchesne brought that emphasis to the USA in 1818. All schools in the Network of Sacred Heart Schools are required to adhere to the Goals and Criteria of the Sacred Heart Education:

1. To educate to a personal and active faith in God.
2. To educate to a deep respect for intellectual values.
3. To educate to a social awareness which impels to action.
4. To educate to the building of community as a Christian value.
5. To educate to personal growth in an atmosphere of wise freedom.

Location and Facilities

Duchesne is located off of I-10 at the corner of Memorial Drive and Chimney Rock. The campus originally covered the 15-acre Bering family estate in 1960, but was reduced by the eventual enlargement of Chimney Rock road. The campus boasts many pine trees and a feeling of seclusion from the Memorial area. Duchesne's facilities include two main classroom buildings, tennis courts, gymnasium, athletics field, and a chapel. The "White House" contains the Lower, Middle, and Upper Schools, as well as the School Libraries. The Fine Arts Building contains an atrium for art shows, a theater room, a dance studio, and several art rooms. The chapel is large enough for 300 people and received multiple awards in 1999 from various religious programs.

Admissions

Students who wish to attend Duchesne must complete their Candidate Profile. The Candidate Profile includes filling out the online application form (available in September 2011), Admissions testing results, Teacher Evaluation forms, all educational records (transcripts & report cards), standardized tests scores, and interviews & visits. Admissions testing for Pre-K to grade 4 students are individualized evaluations, while grades 5 to 12 must submit ISEE test scores. Teacher Evaluation forms for grades 6 to 8 must be from their Math and English teachers, while students in grades 9 to 12 must also include a Teacher Evaluation form from their current principal. Once spaces are filled, Duchesne offers a Wait Pool in which students are not ranked and are reevaluated once a space opens up in enrollment.

Academic Tracks and Curriculum

Duchesne incorporates its Catholic faith and background into all aspects of its curriculum. The school features three tracks: On Track, Advanced Track, and the AP Track. Duchesne requires that students take 4 years of English, Math, Science, History, and Religious Studies in order to graduate. AP courses are listed as electives, but count towards achieving these requirements for each section. As part of the Religious Studies requirements, students must participate in Social Awareness in which they must complete four community service projects each year of their Upper School career. Students may take Robotics and Engineering, World Religions, Creative Writing, Shakespeare, History of Film, Environmental Science, Spanish Literature, and more.

Students must earn 27.5 credits to graduate; one credit equals one year of study: English (4), History (4), Math (4), Science (4), Foreign Language (3), Physical Education/Health (2), Religious Studies (4), Fine Arts (1), Speech (.5), Computer Studies (.5), Laptop Integration (.5), and Social Awareness (no credit).

Special Needs
No information provided.

Foreign Languages
Per graduation requirements, students must take 3 years of a Foreign Language. Duchesne offers French, Spanish, and Latin to satisfy this requirement. The school's history stems from France, and, as such, Duchesne takes pride in its French Language program. Students interested in French may take up to French V, AP French Language, and AP French Literature. Duchesne also offers a comprehensive Spanish Language program, where students may take up to Spanish V, AP Spanish Language, and AP Spanish Literature. Latin I introduces students to the literature and history of Roman culture, and an understanding of the language from which the English language finds many of its roots.

Arts
Students are required to complete 1 credit in Fine Arts courses (most are worth .5 credits) and Duchesne offers a wide selection. Students interested in music may join the Music Ensemble, Sacred Ensemble, Music Theory and Application, Orchestra, and Band, the latter combining with St. Thomas High School for rehearsals performances. Students wishing to get creative with visual media can take courses in Photography, Drawing, Ceramics, and Painting. Theatre Arts courses are also offered for students who wish to develop their acting abilities as well as be exposed to the process of production. Duchesne offers AP Art History and three AP courses in Studio Art (Drawing, 2D Design, and 3D Design).

Technology
Duchesne began the Learning with Laptops program in 1998 and currently offers a 1:1 ratio of computers to students in the Middle and Upper Schools. Students may bring their own laptops or be supplied with a school owned laptop. As of 2010, Duchesne began integrating Tablet PCs into every classroom in grades 5 through 12. DASHBoard (Moodle) is used by students to connect with faculty on matters of homework, tests, and online resources. DASHConnect is the communications portal used to connect parents, Duchesne alum, faculty, and staff. Students may also participate in the CAVE (Computer Audio/Visual Emergencies) Helpdesk, which acts as an internship rather than a traditional class. CAVE Helpdesk students help in the repair of a number of computer and technical issues, from laptops to printers to projection devices. The CAVE staff is certified in the COMPTia A+ curriculum and in Toshiba, IBM, and HP Portables.

Extracurricular Activities
Students in the Upper School have access to a large number of extracurricular activities, such as clubs and opportunities for community service. As for clubs, students may choose one A club, one B club, and one or two Independent clubs, though clubs vary from year to year. A clubs might feature French, Spanish, Tolkien,

and St. Thomas Spirit, while B clubs might feature Face AIDS, Shakespeare, and Anime. Independent clubs might include Fishers of Women, Cycling, Campus Ministry, STAND, Robotics, and Yoga. As part of the Network of Sacred Heart Schools, students have access to the Sacred Heart Exchange Program. This program gives students the opportunity to spend several weeks at another Sacred Heart School in the US or Sprout Creek Farm, a working farm in Poughkeepsie, New York. Students may also attend the Sacred Heart School in Australia during the summer.

Athletics

As early as 7th grade, students can participate in a variety of sports throughout the year, and 8th grade students compete in the Houston Junior Preparatory Conference. 7th and 8th grade students may participate in Basketball, Field Hockey, Cross Country, Soccer, Softball, Swimming, Track, and Volleyball. Upper School students (grades 9-12) compete in the Texas Association of Private and Parochial Schools (TAPPS) league against schools such as St. Agnes and St. Pius. Upper School students may participate in Golf, Basketball, Tennis, Softball, Cross Country, Field Hockey, Soccer, Track, Swimming, and Volleyball. During the summer, Middle and Upper School students may join the Field Hockey and Volleyball camps.

Duchesne Academy Fast Facts

Overview

School Type	Religious, Girls
Religious Affiliation	Roman Catholic
Date Founded	1960
Endowment (June 30, 2010)	$6.3 million
Grades Served	Pre-K to 12th
Enrollment	714
Grade 12	67
Grade 11	62
Grade 10	69
Grade 9	66
Grade 8	56
Grade 7	43
Grade 6	62
Grade 5	48
Grade 4	40
Grade 3	41
Grade 2	40
Grade 1	36
Kindergarten	40
Pre-Kindergarten	44
Student to Teacher Ratio	8:1
Faculty with Advanced Degrees (# / %)	40/73%
Minorities in Student Body	25%

Curriculum

Academic Tracks Offered	On Track, Advanced Track, AP Track
Advanced Placement Courses Offered	16
Languages Offered	French, Spanish, Latin
Calendar (Semester / Trimester / Other)	Semester
Interscholastic Sports Programs	10

Graduating Seniors

National Merit Semi-Finalists (# / %)	1/1%
Average SAT Scores (Class of 2010)	1830
Mathematics	595
Critical Reading	604
Writing	631
% Students Admitted to 4 Year University	N/A

Admissions

Prime Entry Points	Pre-K, K, 1, 5, 9
Pre-K	$11-14,302
Grades K-4	$16,538
Grades 5-8	$18,305
Grades 9-12	$20,047
New Student Fee (Facilities Fund Fee)	$750
PC Tablet Package Fee	~$2,300
Students on Financial Aid	N/A

The Emery/Weiner School

9825 Stella Link, Houston, TX 77025
832-204-5900
www.EmeryWeiner.org

Mr. Stuart Dow, Head of School
Ms. Danny Kahalley, Director of Admissions

History and Overview

The Emery/Weiner School was originally founded as I. Weiner Jewish Secondary School in 1978. In 2001, I. Weiner added the Upper School, or Emery High School, and the schools became known as The Emery/Weiner School. Emery/Weiner graduated its first class of seniors in 2005. Emery/Weiner is accredited by ISAS and SACS and is a part of the Jewish Federation of Greater Houston.

Religious Affiliation

Emery/Weiner is a Jewish day school and incorporates its Jewish faith and background into all aspects of its curriculum. Students attending the Upper School are required to complete 4 years of Judaic Studies as well as 30 hours of community service each year in order to graduate. Emery/Weiner emphasizes *Tikkun Olam*, or "repairing the world," which is a core value in Judaism and refers to community service. Students, parents, and faculty are all requested to be committed to the Ten Commitments, which stress respect and understanding in the Emery/Weiner community and beyond.

Location and Facilities

Emery/Weiner's $14 million campus is located just outside the I-610 Loop, inside the Beltway 8, and on 12 acres of land. Housing over 100,000 square feet of space, the campus features a glass-encased cafeteria, a 500-seat theater, several science and computer labs, art and media studios, a multi-court gymnasium, and library. The Emery/Weiner campus also contains a number of playing fields for the school's athletics programs.

Admissions

Students enrolling with Emery/Weiner must complete the online application form and submit all other required information by mid January. All students must take the ISEE and submit scores to Emery/Weiner. Students entering 10th-12th grade may submit PSAT, SAT, or ACT scores in place of the ISEE. Emery/Weiner accepts students ranging from the 40th percentile to 99th percentile on standardized testing. Students must also submit two teacher recommendation forms (Math and English) as well as official transcripts and school records. Students will participate in an interview with Emery/Weiner's staff and must attend a "shadow" day (either half or full). Along with the online application form, students must fill out a student questionnaire, which is designed so that Emery/Weiner's staff may better understand the applicant.

Academic Tracks and Curriculum

Emery/Weiner follows the definition of curriculum as defined by John Kerr, an educational philosopher (1983), "...all the learning which is planned and guided by the school, whether it is carried on in groups or individually, inside or outside the school." Emery/Weiner features an On Track curriculum and an Advanced Track curriculum. EWS requires students to complete 4 years of English and Judaic Studies, 3 years of History, Math, and Science, and 2 years of Foreign Language, Fine Arts, and Physical Education. The school does not offer certified Advanced Placement courses, as its curriculum does not strictly adhere to the requirements of the College Board. However, students may still sit for AP exams as they are offered and administered on campus.

Students must earn 23 credits and complete 30 hours of community service annually to graduate: English (4), Judaic Studies (4), History (3), Math (3), Science (3), Foreign Language (2), Fine Arts (2), and Physical Education (2).

Special Needs
No information provided.

Foreign Languages
Students must take either Hebrew or Spanish as part of their requirements for graduation from Emery/Weiner, and may take up to Hebrew Advanced: Fluency and Spanish V Advanced. 7th and 8th grade students are given the option of taking Latin as an elective.

Arts
As with every other aspect of Emery/Weiner's curriculum, the Fine Arts are considered to be a part of the student's education. Students have the opportunity to participate in dance, theater arts, music, printmaking, photography, painting, and more. Every spring, the Fine Arts Department at Emery/Weiner presents the Evening of the Arts to showcase the abilities and pieces of a variety of students. Artwork is also featured at the Hope/Kaplan Odyssey Gallery located in the Stein Fine Arts Complex.

Technology
No information provided.

Extracurricular Activities
Emery/Weiner hosts a number of clubs and community service opportunities for its students. Some of the clubs featured at Emery/Weiner include Architecture, Knitting, Trivia, Humane Society, Gay-Straight Alliance, Israel Advocacy, Jewish Student Union, Model UN, and Young Independents. The Tikkun Olam Council is considered the most active of the school's clubs and structures the community service opportunities for much of the school's student body. The Tikkun Olam Council is also charged with planning the community service aspect of the "Winterim Term," where students spend a week participating in community service programs all over Houston.

Athletics
Students are required to fulfill 2 years of Physical Education in the Upper School in order to graduate. Emery/Weiner provides students in the Upper School with the chance to participate in Cross Country, Cheerleading, Six-man Football, Soccer, Basketball, Baseball, Softball, Track & Field, Golf, and Tennis. Students in the Middle School may participate in Soccer, Volleyball, Basketball, Baseball, Softball, Tennis, and Track & Field

Emery/ Weiner Fast Facts

Overview

School Type	Religious, Coeducational
Religious Affiliation	Jewish
Date Founded	1978
Endowment (7/1/2011)	$9.8 million
Grades Served	6th-12th
Enrollment	479
Grade 12	60
Grade 11	72
Grade 10	80
Grade 9	73
Grade 8	65
Grade 7	70
Grade 6	59
Student to Teacher Ratio	8:1
Faculty with Advanced Degrees (# / %)	21/40%
Minorities in Student Body	4%

Curriculum

Academic Tracks Offered	On Track, Advanced Track
Advanced Placement Courses Offered	N/A
Languages Offered	Hebrew, Spanish, Latin
Calendar (Semester / Trimester / Other)	Semester
Interscholastic Sports Programs	10

Graduating Seniors

National Merit Semi-Finalists (# / %)	3/5%
Average SAT Scores (Class of 2010)	N/A
Mathematics	605
Critical Reading	605
Writing	N/A
% Students Admitted to 4 Year University	N/A

Admissions

Prime Entry Points	6, 9
Open House	By Appointment
Application Deadline	January 21st
Grades 6 & 7	$18,050
Grade 8	$19,450
Grades 9-11	$20,825
Grade 12	$20,725
New Student Fee	$2,000
Students on Financial Aid	23%

Episcopal High School

4650 Bissonnet, Bellaire, Texas 77401
713-512-3400
www.EHSHouston.org

Mr. C. Edward Smith, Headmaster
Ms. Audrey Koehler, Director of Admissions

Overview

In 1981, a group of Episcopal parishioners discussed with then Bishop Maurice Benitez that their children often attended day schools at their local churches but that these schools only went through the 8th grade. Therefore, they set about to establish a high school. Their efforts came to fruition just three years later in 1983 when EHS welcomed its first 150 ninth and tenth graders in 1984. The founders purchased a vacant campus from a developer that had formerly served as the home for the Sisters of the Incarnate Word and Blessed Sacrament's convent and high school.

Religious Affiliation

EHS is an institution of the Episcopal Diocese of Texas. As such, one of the school's "four pillars" is religion. Daily chapel attendance in the Episcopal faith is required. Four semesters of religious classes (one semester per year) is also a graduation requirement. Freshmen must take the semester course in the Old Testament. Sophomores must take the semester course in New Testament. Juniors can choose between History of Christianity and World Religions. Seniors must take Ethics and complete a Senior Outreach Project.

Location and Facilities

The school's 35-acre campus is located directly off of the 610 West Loop in the independent, affluent municipality of Bellaire across from Gordon Elementary School. Its campus is bounded on the North by Fournace Place, East by a small road, Avenue B, on the south by Bissonnet St., and the West by the West Loop. The school opened in the renovated buildings of a former convent and high school. In 2001, these buildings were supplemented by a new classroom building, library, student center, gym, track, field house, and stadium complex. EHS is currently fundraising for a new academic and science building and parking garage. The school's athletic facilities include a baseball field, softball field, and three multipurpose fields including a track and field complex.

Admissions

Parents must complete the online application, powered by infosnap, and students must complete the student questionnaire. A photo must be uploaded along with the online application or mailed to EHS separately. Students may schedule ISEE and OLSAT exams with EHS, and the Admission Interview must be completed before February. English and Math Teacher Recommendation Forms and the student's transcripts and records must be submitted by January. The majority of enrollees come from a handful of private middle schools—St. Francis Episcopal Day School, River Oaks Baptist School, Annunciation Orthodox School, and the Presbyterian School.

Academic Tracks and Curriculum

EHS offers three academic tracks—On-Track, Honors, and Advanced Placement. Honors classes begin in the ninth grade. In total the school offers 21 honors classes and 17 Advanced Placement classes. EHS requires two years of a fine art to graduate. Interim Term is the first two weeks in January where all students are required to take one grade-level class and two elective courses. Grade-level classes are chosen by the faculty and recently included themes like "high school survival" for freshman, "[life] choices" for sophomores, and "college application process" for juniors.

The school requires 23 credits to earn a diploma; one credit equals one year of study: English (4), Math (3), Science (3), History (3), Foreign Language (2), Religion (2), Fine Arts (2), Health/ PE (1), Electives (3), Technology (satisfied through laptop program).

Special Needs

One of EHS's guiding principles is to accept students with "average-to-exceptional" abilities. To this extent, the school offers accelerated classes for students who seek greater challenges, but it also provides for students who need extra help in the on-track classes. The Director of Academic Assistance leads the Academic Assistance Program. In this program, accepted students are assigned an Academic Coach who regularly monitors the student's progress and helps them manage his academic load such as scheduling tutorial assistance and monitoring homework performance.

Foreign Languages

EHS requires students to take at least two years of the same foreign language to earn a diploma. The school offers instruction in Chinese, French, Latin, and Spanish. All languages are offered with honors classes and up to the college level. AP classes are offered for French, Latin, and Spanish.

Arts

Students must take at least two years (four semesters) of a fine art to graduate, and EHS offers a wide range of options for them. Students can choose from approximately fifty different classes across five departments—Dance, Music, Visual Arts, Media Arts Communication, and Theatre. Class offerings are diverse and range from the more typical—speech, acting, dance, band, and painting—to the more unique—stage combat, repertory dance, guitar instruction, advanced sculpture, and website design.

Technology

EHS requires all students to bring a laptop to school with them. Its "Laptop Program" makes available computers, wireless access, educational software, and peripherals to all faculty and students. Students may also procure their own laptops but are required to have them. "Computer Technology Proficiency" is a graduation requirement but is fulfilled by the required laptop usage. The school offers numerous elective courses in its technology department including computer programming, graphic design, and website design.

Extracurricular Activities

EHS hosts a number of clubs and organizations that are available to its student body. Examples include the Fit Club, Bowling Knights, Dodge ball Club, Hacky Sack Club, or the Surf Club. For languages, students may join the French, Chinese, Spanish, Latin, or Hebrew Clubs. For the arts, students may join the Art Club or the National Art Honor Society. Students will also have many opportunities with participating in performance art, such as theatrical productions and art retreats.

Athletics

Students are not required to participate in a sport at EHS but athletics is considered one of the school's four pillars. Students are required to participate in two semesters of health and physical education. The school fields interscholastic teams across sixteen sports: baseball, basketball, cheerleading, color guard, cross-country, field hockey, football, golf, lacrosse, soccer, swimming, softball, tennis, track, volleyball, and wrestling. EHS is a member of the Southwest Preparatory Conference.

Episcopal High School Fast Facts

Overview

School Type	Religious, Coeducational
Religious Affiliation	Episcopal
Date Founded	1983
Endowment (June 30, 2010)	$25M
Grades Served	9-12
Enrollment	664
Grade 9	163
Grade 10	175
Grade 11	170
Grade 12	156
Student to Teacher Ratio	7:1
Faculty with Advanced Degrees	61%
Minorities in Student Body	16%

Curriculum

Academic Tracks Offered	On-Track, Honors, AP
Advanced Placement Courses Offered	15
Languages Offered	Chinese, French, Latin, Spanish
Calendar (Semester / Trimester / Other)	Semester
Interscholastic Sports Programs	16

Graduating Seniors

National Merit Semi-Finalists 2011 (# / %)	7 / 4%
Average SAT Scores (Class of 2011)	1738
Mathematics	591
Critical Reading	577
Writing	570
% Students Admitted to 4 Year University	99%

Admissions

Prime Entry Points	9
Grades 9-12	$21,160
New Student Fee	$500
Food Service	$1000
Annual Activity Fee	$325
Annual Technology Fee	$325
Students on Financial Aid	20%

Houston Christian High School

2700 W. Sam Houston, Houston, TX 77043
713-580-6000
www.HoustonChristian.org

Dr. Steve Livingston, Head of School
Carolyn Sparkes, Director of Admissions

Overview

Houston Christian High School split off from Northwest Academy in 1997. It remained on the same campus for two years, and then moved in 1999 to its current location. The school was founded by a group of pastors from several Houston-area evangelical churches. They wanted to create a school which included a focus on Christian values and "spiritual formation;" this continues to be part of the school's mission.

Religious Affiliation

Since its founding, the school has had a strong Christian affiliation. In order for someone to teach at Houston Christian, one must profess belief in the divine inspiration of the Bible, the divinity of Jesus, and the foundations of the Christian faith. This strong Christian focus manifests itself in the curriculum. The school "maintains a Christ-centered environment where Christian principles are integrated throughout all courses." Houston Christian provides Christianity-based courses and requires students to complete a number of Biblical studies classes.

Location and Facilities

Houston Christian High School's 45-acre campus is located on the edge of a residential neighborhood at the intersection of West Sam Houston Tollway N and Kempwood Drive. The school integrates technology into the classrooms and contains a library and writing center. Houston Christian's athletic complex includes a soccer field, fields for lacrosse and field hockey, a stadium, a gym, weight and training rooms, and a cheerleading studio. The school also has a chapel and an outdoor pavilion for events.

Admissions

Houston Christian requires: 1) completed online application; 2) $100 application fee; 3) ISEE scores; 4) Teacher Recommendations from the applicants current Math and English teachers; 5) Report cards from the last three years; 6) Copy of the applicant's birth certificate; and 7) Proof of custody if the applicant's parents are divorced. Standardized test scores beyond the ISEE are optional.

An interview is required and students will be contacted for an interview after submitting their application. Shadowing visits are available, but not required. The student's writing proficiency also plays an important role in the admissions process.

Academic Tracks and Curriculum

Houston Christian offers On Track and AP curriculums. The school offers 18 AP courses, including multiple AP courses in all core subject areas except for Bible. Community service is integrated into Houston Christian's Bible curriculum. Students are required to complete 5 hours of community service for each 9-week grading period. If a student fails to complete five hours of community service, then five points are deducted from the student's quarterly grade in Bible class.

Students must earn 30.5 credits to graduate; one credit equals one year of study. Academic Diploma (2011 and 2012 graduates only): English (4), Math (4), Science (4), Social Studies (4), Bible (4), Computer (1), Fine Arts (1), Electives (6), Speech (1), and PE/Athletics (1.5).

Recommended Diploma: English (4), Math (4), Science (4), Social Studies (4), Bible (4), Computer (1), Fine Arts (1), Electives (4), Speech (1), PE/Athletics (1.5), and Foreign Language (2).

Distinguished AP Diploma: English (4), Math (4), Science (4), Social Studies (4), Bible (4), Computer (1), Fine Arts (1), Electives (3), Speech (1), PE/Athletics (1.5), Foreign Language (3). Students must successfully complete four AP courses for this diploma.

Special Needs

Houston Christian High School has implemented the Program for College Readiness to accommodate the needs of students with learning differences. When students are accepted into this program (which is not guaranteed due to limited space), they are taught according to a multi-tier strategic plan. This includes an individual accommodation plan, communication with parents on all levels, a limited pass/fail option, high teacher-to-student ratios, and a Testing Accommodations Center. However, Houston Christian does not modify its curriculum for individual students. The school only provides accommodations.

Foreign Languages

Houston Christian offers Latin, Mandarin, and Spanish. Foreign language credit is not currently required for graduation, but it is incorporated into the curriculum as an elective. Students graduating in 2013 will be required to complete two years of a foreign language for the Recommended Diploma or three years for the Distinguished AP Diploma. The foreign language department offers two AP courses, both in Spanish.

Arts

Houston Christian High School offers courses in band, choir, orchestra, dance, drama, and the visual arts, as well as a digital music class. The school's Mustang Corral pavilion and the chapel provide venues for fine arts performances, and students in the various divisions of the arts department may have opportunities to show their work or perform for larger audiences, at festivals, or Houston community events. The Houston Christian Fine Arts Council facilitates opportunities for students to perform and showcase their work in off-campus venues.

Technology

All students are required to purchase a MacBook from the school as part of the school's one-to-one laptop initiative. In addition to students' laptops, Mac desktops are available in the library; classrooms at Houston Christian incorporate projectors, printers, document cameras, and SMART Boards.

Extracurricular Activities

Houston Christian has several academic clubs focusing on foreign language, math, and reading. The school has leadership-focused clubs, such as student council, sports-focused clubs, such as the Lacrosse Ladies, and service-centered clubs, such as Young Life and Crochet for Premies. The school also hosts branches of the National Honor Society and the National Art Honor Society.

Athletics

Sports programs are available to students of all grades, and 78% of students participate in these programs. Houston Christian's sports programs compete in TAPPS. Boys have the option of playing baseball and football. Girls have the option of being involved in cheerleading, drill team, field hockey, softball, and volleyball. Both boys and girls may participate in basketball, cross-country, golf, lacrosse, soccer, swimming, tennis, and track.

Houston Christian High School Fast Facts

Overview

School Type	Religious, Coeducational
Religious Affiliation	Christian
Date Founded	1997
Endowment	N/A
Grades Served	9 - 12
Enrollment	485
Grade 12	113
Grade 11	107
Grade 10	136
Grade 9	129
Student to Teacher Ratio	9:1
Faculty with Advanced Degrees (# / %)	N/A
Minorities in Student Body	20%

Curriculum

Academic Tracks Offered	On Track, AP
Advanced Placement Courses Offered	18
Languages Offered	Latin, Mandarin, Spanish
Calendar (Semester / Trimester / Other)	Quarter
Interscholastic Sports Programs	13

Graduating Seniors

National Merit Semi-Finalists (# / %)	11 / 9%
Average SAT Scores (Class of 2012)	1688
Mathematics	N/A
Critical Reading	N/A
Writing	N/A
% Students Admitted to 4 Year University	100%

Admissions

Prime Entry Points	9th Grade
Grades 9-12	$17,430
New Student Fee	$400
Activity Fee	$600
Students on Financial Aid	N/A

The High School for Performing and Visual Arts (HSPVA)

4001 Stanford St., Houston, TX 77006
713-942-1960
www.HSPVA.org

Dr. Scott Allen, Principal
Ms. Marian Mabry, Magnet Coordinator

Overview

HSPVA started in 1971 as a way for young artists and performers to study their disciplines and to prepare for the challenges of competitive arts programs at universities and colleges. As one of the first magnet schools in HISD, HSPVA paved the way for other non-comprehensive high schools to emerge and to offer alternative high school experiences. HSPVA prides itself on fostering creativity and independence while also emphasizing loyalty and responsibility to a community.

Religious Affiliation

As a public school, HSPVA has no religious affiliation. According to Houston Independent School District's policy, every school has a moment of silence each day during which students can pray silently to themselves if they so choose. Also, absences because of religious holidays do not count toward the student's total number of absences. However, the student is still responsible for the makeup work.

Location and Facilities

Currently residing in Montrose, HSPVA sits on what was once Montrose Elementary School. HSPVA moved there in 1981 from its previous location at the corner of Austin St. and Holman St. The current building is two stories and is broken into different sections separating the various arts. HSPVA hosts a recital hall, a black box theatre, and a traditional theatre. The school also includes a dance studio, an art studio, a jazz room, an orchestra room, and a choir room. Numerous practice rooms are spread throughout the school, but students will practice in the hallways from time to time.

Admissions

The HSPVA admissions process includes an application and an audition. All students must fill out the application and submit the following information with it: 1) Most Recent Report Card, 2) Previous Year's Final Report Card, 3) Copy of Transcript/Permanent Record, 4) Two Years of Standardized Test Scores, 5) Copy of Immunization Record, and 6) Proof of HISD Residency. For the Creative Writing fine art category, a portfolio with ten original pieces is due with the application.

For the audition, students can choose two of five possible categories: Creative Writing, Visual Arts, Theatre Arts, Instrumental and Vocal Music, and Dance. Students must rank their choices. The student will have an audition in his or her first choice and will only have an audition in his or her second choice if there are enough available audition times. If the student makes it through the first audition, he or she will be called back for a second audition. A callback is not an offer of admission.

Academic Tracks and Curriculum

HSPVA offers two tracks—On Track and AP. Pre-AP classes lead to 9 classes from the College Board's Advanced Placement (AP) curriculum. HSPVA's AP courses include: AP English Language, AP English Literature, AP Calculus, AP Biology, AP Physics, AP U.S. History, AP Government, AP Economics, and AP Music Theory.

In order to graduate with a Recommended Diploma, students must complete 26 credits; one credit equals one year of study: English (4), Social Studies (4), Math (4), Science (4), Foreign Language (2), Physical Education (1), Speech (1/2), Fine Art (1), and Electives (5 and 1/2). A Distinguished Diploma requires one more year of a foreign language.

Special Needs
Standard HISD policies.

Foreign Languages
HSPVA students must complete at least two years of a foreign language to graduate—three years if the student wishes to earn a Distinguished Diploma. Instruction in two languages is offered—French and Spanish up to Level 4.

Arts
HSPVA students must audition and be admitted in one of five fine art areas in order to attend HSPVA: Creative Writing, Visual Arts, Theatre Arts, Instrumental and Vocal Music, and Dance. Each area has its own requirements. For the Creative Writing Department, the student will take classes in multiple genres, such as poetry, short stories, and drama. The Visual Arts Department includes courses in both traditional art mediums, such as sculpture, as well as computer graphics, such as animation. Not just focusing on acting, the Theatre Arts Department has classes in theatre production, directing, and playwriting. While the Instrumental and Vocal Music Department focuses on a variety of instruments and singing, it also encompasses music literature, music criticism, and music theory classes. The Dance Department offers courses in ballet, modern dance, tap, and jazz.

Technology
HSPVA has one computer lab with thirty computers; however, the only classes allowed to use it are the computer classes. Other subjects may use the library, which holds sixteen desktop computers, or one of two laptop carts, each of which has thirty laptops with wireless internet. HSPVA offers Business Communication Information Systems as a part of its career and technical education department, but a technology credit is no longer required to graduate.

Extracurricular Activities
HSPVA offers a number of different clubs and activities to its students on top of its vigorous fine arts program. Some examples include: Anime Club, Red Cross Club, Literary Magazine, Radio PVA, Hootenanny, Business Professionals of America, Bite and Bike Club, Newspaper, Spanish Honor Society, and National Honor Society. Since the clubs are student oriented, as students' interests change, so do the clubs.

Athletics
Since HSPVA's fine arts curriculum requires so much after school time, HSPVA does not have any official sports teams.

HSPVA Fast Facts

Overview

School Type	Public, Magnet, Coeducational
Religious Affiliation	None
Date Founded	1971
Grades Served	9 - 12
Enrollment	654
Grade 12	151
Grade 11	163
Grade 10	172
Grade 9	152
Student to Teacher Ratio	16:1
Faculty with Advanced Degrees (# / %)	30 / 61 %
Minorities in Student Body	49 %

Curriculum

Academic Tracks Offered	On Track, AP
Advanced Placement Courses Offered	9
Languages Offered	French, Spanish
Calendar (Semester / Trimester / Other)	Semester
Interscholastic Sports Programs	N/A

Graduating Seniors

National Merit Semi-Finalists (# / %)	2 / 1%
Average SAT Scores (Class of 2012)	1676
Mathematics	562
Critical Reading	556
Writing	558
% Students Admitted to 4 Year University	N/A

Public School Stats

Gifted and Talented Students	100%
Free & Reduced Lunch	16%
AYP (2006-2011)	Met AYP
TEA Accountability (2006-2007)	Recognized
TEA Accountability (2007-2013)	Exemplary

Incarnate Word Academy

609 Crawford St., Houston, TX 77002
713-227-3637
www.IncarnateWord.org

Sister Lauren Beck, C.V.I., President
Ms. Sarah Torres, Director of Admissions

Overview

The Congregation of the Sisters of the Incarnate Word and Blessed Sacrament (CVI) founded the Incarnate Word Academy, a girl's college preparatory school, in November of 1873. Although the building has changed, the school remains at its original location at 609 Crawford Street. IWA is accredited by Southern Association of Colleges and Secondary Schools and the Texas Catholic Conference Education Department, and is a member of the National Catholic Education Association.

Religious Affiliation

The Venerable Jeanne de Matel of France founded the Order of the Incarnate Word and Blessed Sacrament in 1625 and part of their mission is "…to serve others with humility, simplicity and charity." Central to the education and ministry of CVI is the Incarnate Word, which refers to Jesus Christ and the core values of His teachings. To those in CVI, Jesus is the embodiment of the Word of God, thus the Incarnate Word. CVI believes that education is one of the most important ways to evangelize the teachings of Jesus Christ, and the school incorporates the Catholic faith into all aspects of their curriculum.

Location and Facilities

Incarnate Word is located in Downtown Houston, primarily within one city block at the corner of Crawford and Capitol streets. Sharing the block with Annunciation Catholic Church, the school is directly opposite Minute Maid Park and two blocks north of Discovery Green Park and the George R. Brown Convention Center. The school has a gym on site but most other athletic facilities are shared with St. Thomas High School.

Admissions

Students interested in applying to IWA must complete the school's application form and submit all necessary information to the school by mail. Available for download from the school's website, the application form includes Principal/Counselor, English Teacher, and Math Teacher Recommendation Forms that must be filled out by the individuals currently occupying those roles for the applicant. Students must also submit an official transcript, standardized test scores, recent report card, and HSPT scores. IWA does accept ISEE scores in place of HSPT scores. The student may also submit a recent photo, but this is optional. Prospective students may arrange with the Director of Admissions to shadow for half a day and experience IWA's classrooms and facilities.

Academic Tracks and Curriculum

IWA features On Track, Honors, Advanced Placement, and Dual Credit curriculums for its students. IWA has partnered with Houston Community College to give students the opportunity to earn college credit in Pre-Calculus, Calculus, Trigonometry, and Psychology. IWA offers six AP courses, which are English Literature, English Language, Spanish Language, Government/Macroeconomics, US History, and Biology. Students attending IWA are required to complete 100 hours of community service, 3 years of a foreign language, and 4 years of theology (which is included in the core curriculum). IWA also requires 4 years of English, Mathematics, and Science in order for a student to graduate.

Special Needs
No information provided.

Foreign Languages
Students must take three years of the same language to graduate. Incarnate Word Academy offers students three options of foreign language courses for study. Students may choose French (up to AP French), Latin (up to AP Latin), and Spanish (up to AP Spanish). The language learning software, Rosetta Stone, is integrated into the Spanish curriculum to provide students with additional practice and feedback.

Arts
IWA includes the study of Fine Arts in its curriculum as well as making available Art and Drama Clubs. Students participating in the Art Club will create a mural by the end of each year to be hung within IWA's campus. Students participating in the Drama Club will perform in a number of plays throughout the year, such as *Annie* and Shakespeare's *Much Ado about Nothing*. In music, students may participate in Band in conjunction with St. Thomas High School's band.

Technology
IWA offers one computer course in order to familiarize its students with basic computer techniques.

Extracurricular Activities
Incarnate Word Academy hosts a number of clubs and organizations in which its students may participate. Students may join clubs such as Chess, Computer, Science, and the Literary Club. Students may also join organizations such as the National Honors Society, Mu Alpha Theta Honors Society, Teens for Unity, and Together Loving Christ. Per IWA's graduation requirements, students must complete 100 hours of community service. In order to achieve this requirement, IWA provides students with a number of service options, such as programs through the Society of St. Vincent de Paul. Acceptable forms of community service must be in direct support of those in need, such as the elderly or handicapped through established organizations or agencies.

Athletics
More than 25% of IWA's student body participates in the school's interscholastic sports program. Incarnate Word is a member of Texas Association of Private and Parochial Schools (TAPPS) in Division 5A and offers nine sports programs. Students may participate in Volleyball, Golf, Cross Country, Basketball, Cheerleading, Soccer, Swimming, Track, and Softball.

Incarnate Word Academy Fast Facts

Overview

School Type	Religious, Girls
Religious Affiliation	Catholic
Date Founded	1873
Endowment	N/A
Grades Served	9th - 12th
Enrollment	262
Grade 12	55
Grade 11	57
Grade 10	72
Grade 9	78
Student to Teacher Ratio	9:1
Faculty with Advanced Degrees (# / %)	14/60%
Minorities in Student Body	66%

Curriculum

Academic Tracks Offered	On Track, Honors, AP, Dual Credit
Advanced Placement Courses Offered	6
Languages Offered	French, Latin, Spanish
Calendar (Semester / Trimester / Other)	Semester
Interscholastic Sports Programs	9

Graduating Seniors

National Merit Semi-Finalists (# / %)	0
Average SAT Scores	N/A
Mathematics	N/A
Critical Reading	N/A
Writing	N/A
% Students Admitted to 4 Year University	90%

Admissions

Prime Entry Points	9th grade
Grades 9-12	$9,600
Student Fee	$400
Registration Fee	$150
Students on Financial Aid	34%

The Kinkaid School

201 Kinkaid Dr., Houston, TX 77024
713-782-1640
www.Kinkaid.org

Mr. Don North, Headmaster
Ms. Iris Bonet, Director of Admissions

Overview

Founded in 1906, The Kinkaid School purports to be the "oldest independent coeducational school in Houston." A public school teacher, Margaret Hunter Kinkaid founded the school when she learned that married women were not allowed to be teachers in her school district. Since its inception, Kinkaid has been based out of three physical locations—Ms. Kinkaid's home, Richmond and Graustark in Montrose, and its current location in Piney Point Village, in the Memorial area of Houston.

Religious Affiliation

Kinkaid is a non-sectarian school and as such equally welcomes students and families of all faiths and those with no professed faiths. However, the school is careful to express its recognition of the importance of faith in its students' lives. Kinkaid's Policy on Religious Expression allows a student to practice their religious traditions before and after school hours and during free time, use school facilities for religious purposes with the Headmaster's permission, and invoke certain religious rituals such as readings and homilies during school events such as graduation when appropriate.

Location and Facilities

Kinkaid's 65-acre campus is located in the city of Piney Point Village, a small enclave of Houston's Memorial area. It is fairly equidistant between Beltway 8, Loop 610, I-10, and the Westpark Tollway. The campus features a densely wooded entrance and is surrounded by an affluent residential neighborhood of single-family homes. Kinkaid embarked on a major construction campaign in the '90s in which about half of the school's 363,000 square feet was newly constructed or rebuilt. Highlights of this campaign included a brand new Lower School, additions to the Middle and Upper schools, new auditorium, and new cafeteria. Athletic facilities include three gymnasiums, baseball field, softball field, batting cages, fitness/ weight room, 1550-seat stadium, and four tennis courts.

Admissions

The Kinkaid admissions process generally includes 1) standardized test scores 2) group testing/ interviews 3) recommendations 4) transcripts. Pre-kindergarten students must be 4 years old by July 1st of their application year. For applicants to the Lower School, the WPPSI standardized test is required for pre-kindergarten through first grade applicants, the WISC for grades 2-4. All applicants are invited to "group testing" where students will interact with teachers. Finally, teacher recommendations and transcripts are required where applicable.

Requirements for grades 5-12 are the same with the exception that the standardized test used is the ISEE. Also, group testing is replaced by interviews for grades 5 and up. Natural entry points, where more admissions slots are available, are pre-kindergarten, kindergarten, grade 6, and grade 9. Preference, not automatic admission, is given to alumni and families with children already enrolled.

Academic Tracks and Curriculum

The Lower School curriculum is self-contained, meaning that students stay in one room while the same group of teachers covers all of the subjects in the curriculum. The Middle and Upper Schools are departmentalized. To facilitate the transition from Lower to Middle School, Kinkaid offers a compulsory Study Skills course. Accelerated curriculum courses are offered beginning in 7th grade. The Upper School offers three tracks—on track, honors, and 14 classes from the College Board's Advanced Placement

(AP) curriculum. Honors sections are not offered for English, History, and Social Studies (AP classes are offered).

The school requires 16 credit hours to graduate; one credit is equivalent to one year of study: English (4), Math (3), Social Studies (3), Science (3), Foreign Languages (2), Fine Arts (1), Computer Studies (general proficiency). Students must also complete 6 out of 12 seasons of Physical Education (including a Health course), a Service credit (1/2), and an Interim Term every January (3 weeks of electives).

Special Needs
No information provided.

Foreign Languages
Foreign language instruction is offered beginning in sixth grade with French and Spanish. An outside contractor provides instruction in Chinese Mandarin after school for Lower School students. Upper School students must complete at least two years of a foreign language to graduate. Instruction in four languages is offered—French up to 5, Spanish up to 5, Latin up to 5, and Chinese up to 3. Preparation for the AP curriculum is offered for Latin, French, and Spanish.

Arts
In the Lower School, music is tightly integrated into the overall curriculum. There is also a one-hour a week Visual Arts class. In the 5th and 6th grades, students rotate through band, orchestra, choir, and visual art. In 7th grade, students meet every other day for speech and debate and are also required to take a music elective and one additional art. 8th grade students have electives of which creative writing is an option. Upper School students must complete at least one year of a fine art elective to graduate. Some of the more notable options include acting, architecture, filmmaking, photography, and yearbook. Speech and debate is included in the art requirement at Kinkaid. Kinkaid also has an Upper School band and orchestra that often travel both inside and outside the country for competitions and performances.

Technology
Kinkaid has over 130 mostly Mac computers in classrooms, mobile, and desktop labs. iPads are used in kindergarten. Middle Schoolers use iMovie to create "Life Stories," and Upper Schoolers learn how to program for the iPhone. Graduation from Upper School is contingent on the successful completion of the Kinkaid Technology Requirement. Students fulfill the requirement by either successfully completing a computer course or through an independent project. The school utilizes an intranet powered by Moodle. Students are not required to bring laptops to class.

Extracurricular Activities
Lower School and Middle School students may participate in student government activities. The Upper School government includes a mix of elected students and faculty. There is a literary magazine for the Middle School and yearbook for Middle and Upper Schools. Students in the Upper School may also participate in the school's newspaper.

Athletics
Students are not required to participate in a sport at Kinkaid but 100% of Middle School students and 80% of Upper School students usually participate in at least one sport according to the school. The school fields more than fifty teams across fifteen sports: baseball, basketball, cheerleading, cross-country, field hockey, football, golf, lacrosse, soccer, swimming, softball, tennis, track, volleyball, and wrestling. Kinkaid is a member of the Southwest Preparatory Conference.

The Kinkaid School Fast Facts

Overview

School Type	Independent, Coeducational
Religious Affiliation	None
Date Founded	1906
Endowment (reported on 7/31/10)	$79.4M
Grades Served	Pre-K - 12
Enrollment	1366
Grade 12	136
Grade 11	135
Grade 10	137
Grade 9	138
Grade 8	110
Grade 7	111
Grade 6	118
Grade 5	72
Grade 4	72
Grade 3	72
Grade 2	73
Grade 1	72
Kindergarten	72
Pre-Kindergarten	48
Student to Teacher Ratio	9:1
Faculty with Advanced Degrees (# / %)	74/60%
Minorities in Student Body	19%

Curriculum

Academic Tracks Offered	On Track, Honors, AP
Advanced Placement Courses Offered	14
Languages Offered	Chinese, French, Latin, Spanish
Calendar (Semester / Trimester / Other)	Semester
Interscholastic Sports Programs	15

Graduating Seniors

National Merit Semi-Finalists 2011 (# /%)	9/7%
Average SAT Scores (Class of 2011)	1948
Mathematics	661
Critical Reading	641
Writing	646
% Students Admitted to 4 Year University	100

Admissions

Prime Entry Points	Pre-K, K, 6, 9
Pre-K and Kindergarten	$16,000
Grades 1-4	$16,540
Grades 5-8	$19,140
Grades 9-12	$20,530
New Student Fee	$1000
Books and Supplies	~$600
Students on Financial Aid	N/A

Lamar High School

3325 Westheimer, Houston, TX 77098
713-522-5960
www.LamarHS.org

Dr. James McSwain, Principal

Overview

In 1859, a school for local children opened at what, in 1936, would become Lamar High School. Forty-six years later, Lamar added its IB program, and seven years after that, it added its Business Magnet Program. Lamar serves River Oaks, the incorporated city of West University Place, and other Houston subdivisions. Lamar's mission is to create an atmosphere of "shared responsibility, academic challenge, intercultural understanding, and mutual respect."

Religious Affiliation

As a public school, Lamar has no religious affiliation. According to Houston Independent School District's policy, every school has a moment of silence each day during which students can pray silently to themselves if they so choose. Also, absences because of religious holidays do not count toward the student's total number of absences. However, the student is still responsible for the makeup work.

Location and Facilities

Currently residing in Upper Kirby, Lamar sits at Westheimer and Buffalo Speedway. Lamar has four buildings, three of which are connected by second story crosswalks. The North Building contains mostly administrative offices and classrooms, while the West Building contains science and computer labs and the East Building contains the library and theatre. The school also has a performance hall, a traditional theatre, and a natatorium (a building containing a swimming pool).

Admissions

Lamar's admissions process is split into two different types: zoned and magnet. However, all students need the following documents in order to register: 1) Student's Birth Certificate, 2) Proof of Custody (if applicable), 3) Copy of Transcript/Permanent Record, 4) Copy of Immunization Record, and 5) Proof of HISD Residency.

For the Business Administration Magnet Program, all students must fill out the magnet application and submit the following information with it: 1) First 6-week Report for 8th Grade, 2) Previous Year's Final Report Card, 3) Copy of Transcript/Permanent Record, 4) Standardized Test Scores, 5) Proof of HISD Residency.

Note that even if the student is zoned for Lamar, the student needs to apply for the magnet program in order to participate in it.

If accepted, students must attend a three-week Summer Academy in June, and all magnet students automatically participate in the IB program. Only incoming 9th graders are accepted.

Academic Tracks and Curriculum

Lamar offers three tracks—On Track, Dual-Credit, and AP/IB. Pre-IB classes lead to the 30 IB classes. Lamar offers only two AP courses: AP Calculus AB and AP Statistics. Lamar currently has a partnership with Houston Community College that allows Lamar to offer its dual-credit track where students can get credit for English IV, college algebra, government, economics, and psychology from Houston Community College.

As well as its Business Magnet Program, Lamar also offers a variety of career pathways, including culinary arts, engineering, agriculture, communications, business, health science, marine biology, and government.

In order to graduate with an IB Diploma, students are required to complete six subjects, three Higher Level and three Standard Level courses. These subjects include: first language, second language, math, science, social science, and an IB elective. Students must also complete 150 hours of CAS (community, action, and service), a 4,000-word research essay, and a capstone course titled Theory of Knowledge.

In order to graduate with a Recommended Diploma, students must complete 26 credits; one credit equals one year of study: English (4), Social Studies (4), Math (4), Science (4), Foreign Language (2), Physical Education (1), Speech (1/2), Fine Art (1), and Electives (5 and 1/2). A Distinguished Diploma requires one more year of a foreign language.

Special Needs
No school specific information provided outside of general HISD policies.

Foreign Languages
Lamar offers courses in eight languages: French, German, Hebrew, Italian, Japanese, Russian, Spanish, and Mandarin. Every language goes through level 4 except for French, German, Russian, Spanish, and Mandarin, which go through level 5. Non-magnet students must complete at least two years of a foreign language to graduate—three years if the student wishes to earn a Distinguished Diploma.

Arts
Lamar students must complete at least one year of a fine art elective to graduate. The options include band, dance, music, orchestra, art, choir, and theatre arts. University Interscholastic League (UIL) sponsors the choir, so it participates in competitions against other schools through the UIL. However, every fine art department at Lamar has won accolades.

Technology
In its multiple computer labs, Lamar offers Business Computer Information Systems, Pre-IB Computer Science, IB Computer Science, Computer Aided Drafting, Magnet Business Image Management and Multimedia, and Desktop Publishing as a part of its career and technical education department.

Extracurricular Activities
Lamar offers a number of different clubs and activities to its students. Some examples include: Academic Decathlon, Quill & Scroll, Odyssey of the Mind, Yearbook, Lamar Animal Welfare Society, Ping Pong Club, Breakfast Club, and Cheerleading.

Athletics
Lamar has fifteen sports teams, including: football, baseball, softball, volleyball, field hockey, wrestling, golf and boys' and girls' basketball, lacrosse, soccer, track, cross-country, tennis, water polo, and swimming. Athletic facilities include tennis courts, baseball fields, running track, football fields, basketball courts, and gun range.

Lamar High School Fast Facts

Overview

School Type	Public, Magnet, Coeducational
Religious Affiliation	None
Date Founded	1936
Grades Served	9-12
Enrollment	3003
Grade 12	650
Grade 11	792
Grade 10	670
Grade 9	891
Student to Teacher Ratio	18:1
Faculty with Advanced Degrees (#/%)	64/39%
Minorities in Student Body	66%

Curriculum

Academic Tracks Offered	On Track, Dual Credit, IB
International Baccalaureate Courses	30
Languages Offered	IB languages including: French, German, Russian, Italian, Spanish, Japanese, Mandarin, Hebrew
Calendar (Semester / Trimester / Other)	Semester
Interscholastic Sports Programs	15

Graduating Seniors

National Merit Semi-Finalists (#/%)	3/0.5%
Average SAT Scores (Class of 2012)	1515
Mathematics	514
Critical Reading	508
Writing	493
% Students Admitted to 4 Year University	N/A

Public School Stats

Gifted and Talented Students	25%
Free & Reduced Lunch	45%
AYP (2006-2011)	Met AYP
TEA Accountability (2006-2007)	Academically Acceptable
TEA Accountability (2007-2013)	Recognized

Lanier Middle School

2600 Woodhead Street, Houston, TX 77098
713-942-1900
www.PurplePups.org

Ms. Linda Smith, Principal
Ms. Aurora Terry, IB/Magnet Coordinator

Overview
Lanier Junior High School was founded in 1926 as one of the first junior high schools in HISD and was named after Southern poet Sidney Lanier. Lanier occupies its original building, although it has undergone many renovations to upgrade its existing facilities. Lanier's mission is to "provide a relevant rigorous academic curriculum in order to encourage students to become self-directed lifelong learners who are innovative problem solvers, effective communicators, open minded thinkers, and caring participants in their local and global communities."

Religious Affiliation
As a public school, Lanier Middle School has no religious affiliation. According to Houston Independent School District's policy, every school has a moment of silence each day during which students can pray silently to themselves if they so choose. Also, absences because of religious holidays do not count toward the student's total number of absences. However, the student is still responsible for the makeup work.

Location and Facilities
Lanier's campus at 2600 Woodhead includes a three story main building, a separate building for band and drama, and two temporary buildings for leadership, debate, and health. An auditorium is located in the center of the campus. Athletic facilities consist of an indoor pool in the basement and an all-purpose sports field behind the main building. The main building and the campus have undergone many renovations since the school's opening in 1926, most recently in 2008/2009, but there are no current plans for future renovation. The surrounding neighborhood consists of an eclectic group of single-family homes, as well as small shops, bars, and restaurants.

Admissions
Lanier's Vanguard Magnet/GT Program requires 1) completed application; 2) final report card averages; 3) Teacher Recommendation form; 4) Naglieri test results (NNAT); and 5) Stanford test results. For students coming from a private school or a school outside of HISD, an appointment must be made for GT testing. All applicants who have met the requirements are placed into a lottery from which approximately 275 students are selected to be a part of the program. The remainder of applicants will be placed on a waiting list.

Academic Tracks and Curriculum
Lanier features three curriculums: On-Track, a Vanguard Magnet/GT, and an IB Middle Years Program (IBMYP). Lanier is the only middle school in HISD that hosts an authorized IBMYP. The five-year IB program is designed to prepare students for the IB program at Lamar High School, with three years at Lanier (sixth through eighth grade) and two years at Lamar (eleventh and twelfth grade). Students in the IBMYP are required to take English, math, science, fine art, technology, physical education, and a second language. Lanier's Vanguard Magnet/GT program is designed to complete the regular sixth through eighth grade track in two years. Students' eighth grade year will focus on high school credit courses.

Special Needs
Standard HISD policies.

Foreign Languages

Lanier offers Spanish, French, German, and Mandarin Chinese. As part of the IB program, students must take a course in a second language.

Arts

Lanier hosts five fine arts programs: band, choir, dance, drama, and orchestra. These arts programs compete in a variety of competitions throughout the state and have won numerous awards.

Technology

Students are prohibited from bringing electronic devices onto campus, with the exception of cell phones, which must be kept in lockers during school hours. Computers are available during supervised class time.

Extracurricular Activities

Lanier offers a number of extracurricular clubs and activities, including: Speech and Debate, Drama, Art/Media Kids, Robotics, Chess Club, Model United Nations, Photography, Fiction Club, Geography Club, National Junior Honors Society, Band, Cheerleading, Drill Team, Name that Book, Ladies of Lanier, Breakdancing, Student Council, Orchestra, Yearbook, Continental Math League, MathCOUNTS, and Visual/Media Arts. Some clubs meet during a 40-minute time period during the school day on Friday.

Athletics

Students are not required to participate in Lanier's afterschool sports program. The school offers both University Interscholastic League and club sports, including baseball, boys and girls basketball, cross country, football, boys and girls soccer, swimming, track and field, volleyball, and softball.

Lanier Middle School Fast Facts

Overview

School Type	Public, Vanguard, Coeducational
Religious Affiliation	N/A
Date Founded	1926
Grades Served	6 – 8
Enrollment	1,336
Grade 8	451
Grade 7	463
Grade 6	422
Student to Teacher Ratio	18:1
Faculty with Advanced Degrees	29/38%
Minorities in Student Body	58%

Curriculum

Academic Tracks Offered	On-Track, Vanguard Magnet/GT, IB
Languages Offered	Spanish, French, German, Mandarin Chinese
Calendar (Semester / Trimester / Other)	Semester
Interscholastic Sports Programs	11

Public School Stats

Gifted and Talented Students	66%
Free & Reduced Lunch	33%
AYP (2006-2011)	Met AYP
TEA Accountability (2006-2013)	Recognized

Pershing Middle School

3838 Blue Bonnet Blvd., Houston, TX 77025
713-295-5240
www.PershingMS.org

Ms. Robin Lowe, Principal
Ms. Rachel Burgan, Magnet Coordinator

Overview

Pershing Middle School was established as part of HISD in 1928. Originally connected to West University Elementary School, Pershing moved to its own campus in 1948 on Braes Boulevard. It has since been rebuilt at the same location but with a new address on Blue Bonnet St. Pershing's mission statement is "to educate all students in a safe, enriched, learning environment, to become responsible, productive citizens in an ever-changing society."

Religious Affiliation

As a public school, Pershing Middle School has no religious affiliation. According to Houston Independent School District's policy, every school has a moment of silence each day during which students can pray silently to themselves if they so choose. Also, absences because of religious holidays do not count toward the student's total number of absences. However, the student is still responsible for the makeup work.

Location and Facilities

The campus is located at 3838 Blue Bonnet Boulevard. Facilities include a baseball field, an all-purpose sports field, one main building and a smaller auxiliary building. Between 2005 and 2007 the entire school was rebuilt. Braeswood Place, the neighborhood surrounding Pershing, is a largely residential area close to West University Place, Southside Place, and Bellaire.

Admissions

Pershing's Fine Arts Magnet requires that applicants 1) complete and submit an application; 2) submit the most recent report card and test records and last year's report card; 3) permanent record/transcript; 4) immunization record; 5) proof of HISD residency; and 6) guardian's photo ID. Prior to application, students must have maintained an overall grade point average of 78 or higher, good conduct, and good attendance. Students must also have experience or demonstrate potential in fine arts. If the applicant meets the requirements, the school will then send a letter with a specified audition time, and the auditions will be ranked. Students may choose one of the following: band, orchestra, choir, art, dance, gymnastics, guitar, or theater arts.

Pershing's Neighborhood Vanguard GT Program requires 1) completed application; 2) previous year's final report card; 3) end of semester report card; 4) Teacher Recommendation Form; 5) achievement test scores (Stanford/Aprenda); 6) current Naglieri non-verbal Ability Test-2 results; and 7) proof of HISD residency. The applicant may be required to complete extra testing, but this will be scheduled by the GT coordinator.

Academic Tracks and Curriculum

Pershing has three academic tracks: On-Track, Pre-AP, and Pre-AP/GT. The Pre-AP/GT curriculum includes Language Arts, Mathematics, Language other than English, Science, Social Studies/History, and Speech. Seventh and eighth grade students in the Pre-AP/GT program will have the option of choosing Spanish, French, or Mandarin Chinese to fulfill their language requirement. Eighth grade students in the Pre-AP/GT program will take Algebra I and Integrated Physics and Chemistry (IPC). In 2014, eighth grade students will have the opportunity to take Geometry.

Special Needs
Standard HISD policies.

Foreign Languages
Pershing offers French, Spanish, and Mandarin Chinese. Spanish speakers may qualify to take Spanish AP language classes during 8th grade and can earn up to four high school credits.

Arts
Students in Pershing's Fine Arts Magnet program select one area of concentration: visual art, band, dance, theater arts, choir, orchestra, gymnastics, or guitar. Each program has a variety of performances and exhibitions, both mandatory and optional, throughout the year. The school runs a blog dedicated to posting both art and performance schedules.

Technology
Students are not allowed to use laptops or their other unnecessary electronics during school. Computer labs are available for schoolwork.

Extracurricular Activities
Numerous clubs are available both before and after classes: BETA club, Bluebonnet Street Journal, Booster, Chess, Cheerleading, Club de Espanola, Drama club, Math Counts, Name that Book, NJHS, No Place For Hate, Odyssey of the Mind, Perfect ten Step team, Prep Bowl, Robotics, Spanish Book Club, and Student Council. The school hosts these programs, but YMCA after-school programs with enrichment and athletic activities are available and encouraged.

Athletics
After-school sports are available throughout the year. Boys' teams are baseball, basketball, cross-country, football, lacrosse, soccer, and swimming. Girls' sports are basketball, softball, cheerleading, cross-country, lacrosse, and volleyball.

Pershing Middle School Fast Facts

Overview

School Type	Public, Magnet, Coeducational
Religious Affiliation	N/A
Date Founded	1928
Grades Served	6 – 8
Enrollment	1,748
Grade 8	597
Grade 7	641
Grade 6	510
Student to Teacher Ratio	17:1
Faculty with Advanced Degrees (# / %)	29/28%
Minorities in Student Body	81%
Students Receiving Free / Reduced Lunch	53%

Curriculum

Academic Tracks Offered	On-Track, Pre-AP, Pre-AP/GT
Advanced Placement Courses Offered	N/A
Languages Offered	Spanish, French, Mandarin
Calendar (Semester / Trimester / Other)	Semester
Interscholastic Sports Programs	10

Public School Stats

Gifted and Talented Students	26%
Free & Reduced Lunch	53%
AYP (2006-2011)	Met AYP
TEA Accountability (2006-2009)	Academically Acceptable
TEA Accountability (2009-2013)	Recognized

Pin Oak Middle School

4601 Glenmont, Bellaire, TX 77401
713-295-6500
www.PinOak.us

Ms. Susan Monaghan, Principal
Ms. Cindy Cook, Magnet Coordinator

Overview
Founded in 2002, Pin Oak Middle School is an "application only" school, meaning that no students are zoned for it; every student must apply. Pin Oak includes a Vanguard program for Gifted/Talented students and a foreign language magnet. Pin Oak also has a house system where students are assigned a house and belong to it their three years at Pin Oak. House C is reserved for the foreign language magnet students.

Religious Affiliation
As a public school, Pin Oak has no religious affiliation. According to Houston Independent School District's policy, every school has a moment of silence each day during which students can pray silently to themselves if they so choose. Also, absences because of religious holidays do not count toward the student's total number of absences. However, the student is still responsible for the makeup work.

Location and Facilities
Residing next to the 610 loop and US 59 in Bellaire, Pin Oak is surrounded by West University neighborhoods. Its main, 174,500 square foot building rests on eighteen acres of land that once housed horses. As a result, Pin Oak tries to include horses in much of its activities, such as making its mascot a charger.

Admissions
Pin Oak's admissions process can be split into two categories: neighborhood program and magnet program.

For the neighborhood program, any student residing in the zoned areas for Jane Long, Johnston, or Pershing Middle Schools can apply. Pin Oak then uses a lottery to determine acceptance. In order to apply to Pin Oak, the parent needs to file for a Boundary Option Transfer with the school.

For the foreign language magnet program, any student within the boundaries of HISD may apply, including the students in the above-mentioned zoned areas. Parents must submit 1) an application, 2) the student's final report card from the previous year, 3) the first cycle report card of the current year, 4) standardized test results, 5) proof of residency, 6) immunization records, and 7) a permanent record/transcript. Pin Oak uses students' academic histories to determine acceptance into the magnet program.

All students admitted to Pin Oak may apply for the Vanguard program by filling out an application.

Academic Tracks and Curriculum
Pin Oak offers Pre-AP and G/T classes for the core subjects: foreign language, English, history, math, and science. In addition to the core subjects, Pin Oak offers courses in drama, guitar, chorale, art, orchestra, photography, and life skills, to name a few.

Special Needs
No school specific information provided outside of general HISD policies.

Foreign Languages
Pin Oak offers foreign language class in Chinese, French, Italian, Latin, Hebrew, and Spanish. Students in the magnet program complete one year of high school foreign

language credit unless they opt for the native speaker's tract where they can earn two years of high school foreign language credit. Native Spanish speakers have the opportunity to earn four years of high school foreign language credit if they complete Native Speaker's 1 and the AP Spanish Language courses.

Arts

Pin Oak's fine arts program includes: band, orchestra, choir, dance, theater, and visual arts. Pin Oak has received awards for its choir, and its orchestra performs charity shows around Houston.

Technology

No information provided.

Extracurricular Activities

Pin Oak offers more than 50 student clubs, including Young Ladies in Training, No Place For Hate, Arts and Crafts, Golf, Movie Club, Jewelry Club, and Student Council.

Athletics

Pin Oak's boys' sports include football and baseball while the girls' sports include volleyball. Both boys and girls can participate in cross-country, swimming, basketball, soccer, lacrosse, and track. Pin Oak's athletic facilities include two baseball diamonds, a football field, two soccer fields, and three tennis courts. Although it does not have a swimming pool, Pin Oak uses the pool at Johnston Middle School.

Pin Oak Middle School Fast Facts

Overview

School Type	Public, Magnet, Coeducational
Religious Affiliation	None
Date Founded	2002
Grades Served	6th-8th
Enrollment	1153
6th Grade	394
7th Grade	397
8th Grade	362
Student to Teacher Ratio	17:1
Faculty with Advanced Degrees (# / %)	27 / 38%
Minorities in Student Body	68%

Curriculum

Academic Tracks Offered	Pre-AP, G/T
International Baccalaureate Courses	N/A
Languages Offered	Chinese, French, Italian, Latin, Hebrew, Spanish
Calendar (Semester / Trimester / Other)	Semester
Interscholastic Sports Programs	9

Public School Stats

Gifted and Talented Students	50%
Free & Reduced Lunch	35%
AYP (2006-2011)	Met AYP
TEA Accountability (2006-2007)	Recognized
TEA Accountability (2007-2013)	Exemplary

Post Oak Montessori School

4600 Bissonnet Street, Bellaire, TX 77007   Mr. John Long, Head of School
713-661-6688   Ms. Vivian Blum, Admission Director
www.PostOakSchool.org

History
Founded in 1963, Post Oak School was Houston's first AMI Montessori school, serving children between the ages of 3 and 6. Since 1980, the school has increased its age range to include children in pre-K through eighth grade. In the fall of 2012, Post Oak will expand once again to include children in high school. Post Oak Montessori School is among over 5,000 Montessori schools nationwide established based on Dr. Montessori's ideas and educational methods. The school was originally located at a house on Briar Ridge Drive but has since relocated to the school's current building, which was custom-built for its use and purposes in 1986.

Religious Affiliation
Post Oak is a non-sectarian school, and as such equally welcomes students and families of all faiths and those with no professed faiths. The school accepts qualified students regardless of religion.

Location and Facilities
Post Oak Montessori School is located in the city of Bellaire, a suburb of Houston, Texas. The campus occupies a 3.44-acre lot located at the intersection of Bissonnet and Avenue B and is accessible from the rest of the urban area, as the highway I-610 passes nearby. Built in 1986, the school occupies approximately 55,279 square feet and includes 19 classrooms as well as rooms for primary home environment and elementary before-and-after care. Each classroom offers a complete set of customized furniture created for the specific uses of the children working in that environment. The school is also equipped with a full gym and backfield, which is utilized by the school's Bearkats athletic teams.

Admissions
The Post Oak School admissions process generally includes 1) a campus tour, 2) a written application, 3) a transcript, 4) an interview, and 5) a teacher recommendation. An electronic version of the application is available for view; however, electronic applications will not be accepted in admissions considerations. Applicants are given priority in the following order: qualified siblings of students currently attending the Post Oak School, applicants whose parents previously attended the Post Oak School parent education programs, and all other applicants. Children are age eligible to enter the infant community if they will be between the ages of 14 months and 24 months at the start of the school year. The school recommends that parents enroll their children as early as possible in order to take advantage of the sensitive learning period between birth and the age of five. Post Oak desires students who are respectful of all adults and children, the school, and the school's programs.

Academic Tracks and Curriculum
The Post Oak School utilizes the Montessori educational method, which was developed by an Italian physician, Maria Montessori, and serves children from birth to the age of eighteen. The Montessori Method emphasizes independence and freedom within limits and takes into account the variation of behavioral tendencies of children of different ages. It involves mixed age classrooms, student choice of activity, and uninterrupted periods of work.

At the high school level, students will study English language arts, history and the humanities, science, math, foreign language, PE, and the fine arts, as prescribed by the International Baccalaureate Diploma program.

In order to graduate with an IB Diploma, students are required to complete six subjects, three Higher Level and three Standard Level courses. These subjects include: first language, second language, math, science, social science, and an IB elective. Students must also complete 150 hours of CAS (community, action, and service), a 4,000-word research essay, and a capstone course titled Theory of Knowledge.

Special Needs
No information provided.

Foreign Languages
Post Oak School offers ASEP (After School Enrichment Program) classes in which students can learn foreign languages. Both Chinese and Spanish classes are offered through the ASEP program for lower and upper elementary students. In addition, many classroom assistants and teachers are fluent in Spanish and include it as an integral part of daily classroom life. Younger classes concentrate on basic vocabulary and conversation while older students learn Spanish grammar, verb conjugations, and written Spanish.

Arts
In both elementary and middle school, the students explore a variety of artistic media, including drawing, painting, and sculpting. Included in their exploration of art, students also learn about art history and the inclusion of culture into art. Each class plans and produces an art project for Post Oak's biennial Gala. In addition, older classes design the sets for classroom theatrical productions. For lower and upper elementary students, the Post Oak School also offers optional art programs after school through their ASEP (After School Enrichment Program). In this program, students are introduced to various methods of painting, including watercolors, pastels, acrylics, and mixed media approaches.

Technology
At the Post Oak School, all classrooms are fully equipped with technology and technological support to assist the teachers in teaching their students. The library provides an additional four computers to which students have access for educational purposes. Computers are utilized on a regular basis, and the use of technology is integrated into the learning environment. The use of personal laptops and computers is not permitted on the Post Oak campus unless individual permission has been granted.

Extracurricular Activities
The Post Oak School offers several optional after school classes, including Art, Choir, Chinese, Spanish, and Chess classes. A variety of clubs are also offered for student participation, including cheer squad, Montessori Model UN, stamp collecting, running club, and dance.

Athletics
For students in middle school, the Post Oak School offers cross-country and volleyball in the fall as well as basketball in the winter. Each sport is divided into a boy's team and girl's team. For students in elementary school, an intramurals sports squad is offered during the fall and winter. During the season, practices occur on Tuesday, Wednesday, and Thursday afternoons. In the spring, a post-season flag football team is offered for students in both elementary and middle school.

Post Oak Montessori School Fast Facts

Overview

School Type	Montessori, Coeducational
Religious Affiliation	Nonsectarian
Date Founded	1963
Endowment	N/A
Grades Served	Pre-K – 12
Enrollment	365
Upper School (Grades 9-12)	0 (begins 2012)
Grade 8	9
Grade 7	16
Grade 6	11
Grade 5	21
Grade 4	27
Grade 3	27
Grade 2	33
Grade 1	33
Kindergarten	35
Pre-Kindergarten	153
Student to Teacher Ratio	9:1
Faculty with Advanced Degrees (# / %)	N/A
Minorities in Student Body	25%

Curriculum

Academic Tracks Offered	IB
International Baccalaureate Courses	N/A
Languages Offered	Chinese, Spanish
Calendar (Semester / Trimester / Other)	N/A
Interscholastic Sports Programs	3

Graduating Seniors

National Merit Semi-Finalists (# / %)	N/A
Average SAT Scores (Class of 2010)	N/A
Mathematics	N/A
Critical Reading	N/A
Writing	N/A
% Students Admitted to 4 Year University	N/A

Admissions

Prime Entry Points	Pre-K, 1, 9
Pre-K and Kindergarten	$12,900-$21,200
Grades 1-8	$16,100
Grades 9-12	$21,000
New Student Fee	$500
Travel Fee	$3000
Students on Financial Aid	N/A

Presbyterian School of Houston

5300 Main Street, Houston, Texas 77004
713-520-0284
www.pshouston.org

Dr. Mark Carleton, Headmaster
Kristin Brown, Director of Admission

Overview

Presbyterian School of Houston was founded in 1988 and received its first class of students in 1989. In August 2000, the school expanded with its addition of a middle school and accepted its first class of fifth and sixth graders. Presbyterian graduated its first class of eighth grade students in 2003. The mission of "Family, School and Church united in the Education and support of each Child" is the founding premise upon which Presbyterian School continues to nurture and challenge its students.

Religious Affiliation

Presbyterian was founded on the belief that students should be educated in an environment integrating the three most important institutions in life: family, school, and the Church. Students are encouraged to develop their spiritual identities in a Christ-centered environment, as well as a sense of responsibility in relation to God. However, students of all religious backgrounds are welcome to attend Presbyterian. All students attend Chapel once a week. In addition to weekly chapel, several all-community chapel services are held to unite the community, mark important events and manifest the Christian foundation of Presbyterian School.

Location and Facilities

Presbyterian School has two campuses: a main campus and an outdoor education campus. The main campus is located in a facility owned by First Presbyterian Church of Houston in the heart of Houston's museum district. The main campus includes modern facilities with two learning commons, three science labs, two art rooms including an in-house kiln, two music rooms, an Academic Enrichment Center, computer lab, and a 1200-seat theatre to accommodate over 500 students. The outdoor education campus is located less than 5 miles from the main campus and includes 14 acres of outdoor space for environmental learning, three rock-climbing walls, two gymnasiums sports and athletics, nature trails, and outdoor worship.

Admissions

Students applying to Presbyterian School of Houston must complete 1) an online application, 2) a school visit, 3) admissions testing, 4) Teacher Recommendation forms, and 5) an official school transcript. Pre-K and Kindergarten students must take the WPPSI-III and participate in a group visit to the school with other applicants. First grade to fourth grade students must take the WISC-IV, and will participate in a group visit with other applicants. Fifth through eighth grade students must take the ISEE and OLSAT and shadow a middle school student for an afternoon. Sixth through eighth grade must acquire teacher recommendation forms from their current math and English teachers.

Academic Tracks and Curriculum

Early Childhood students explore ideas and develop skills through art, music and movement, dramatic play, blocks, language arts, social studies, and math. Field trips, interactive science experiments, and readiness activities in reading and math further enhance the program. Small and full group work sparks curiosity and creativity, and encourages children to observe, experiment, solve problems, and acquire basic skills. Lower School students are taught Language Arts, *Everyday Mathematics*, and Social Studies in their primary classroom. Faculty with specialized training in Science, Art, Chapel, Computer, Library, Music, Physical Education, and Spanish provide instruction beyond the walls of a student's homeroom and in interdisciplinary activities. Middle School students are required to take English, History, Mathematics,

Science, Spanish, and Physical Education classes. Rotation classes are also required for students in each grade, which include Art, Religion, Music, and Study Skills. Presbyterian provides wellness electives for students in seventh and eighth grade, such as wellness classes, strength and cardio classes, recreational games, and study hall. 7th and 8th grade students take an exam at the end of the second and fourth quarters.

Special Needs
No information on special needs programs.

Foreign Languages
For elementary school students, Spanish is taught through immersion instruction with emphasis placed on recognition and production of Spanish vocabulary. In upper elementary school, students begin learning Spanish grammar, reading, and writing. In middle school, students continue studying Spanish grammar, reading, and writing as well as practicing spoken Spanish.

Fine Arts
Presbyterian School offers an art program focusing on the principles of design and aesthetic awareness, as well as art history. Prekindergarten to 8th grade students go to Art and Music class each week. Students also have opportunity for public performances through class plays (i.e. Kindergarten Circus), school wide programs (i.e. Lower School Poetry Program) or grade level productions (i.e. 8th grade musical). For students who wish to have additional music classes beyond the school day, they may join one of the School's five choirs.

Supplementing the School's art program are strategic partnerships that occur during the school day with neighboring institutions of Arts. Early Childhood students walk across the street to the Museum of Fine Arts for story time each week. Lower School students walk across the street to the Glassell School of Art for art classes. Middle School faculty are partnering with the Museum of Fine Arts to help them develop middle school art curriculum. A Director of Fine Arts has been appointed in 2012 to continue developing the School's strategic vision of enhancing the Arts at the School.

Technology
Presbyterian School is a completely wireless campus. Parents, students and faculty can access the wireless technology on any given device (iPad, laptop, desk top, smartphone, etc.) Faculty are welcome to bring their own technology to use in the School. In a continuing effort to give teachers the best possible resources for their own growth, all faculty will be given an iPad for their personal and professional use. In addition, the school is asking teachers to study, research, and create programs and initiatives with this technology that will resonate with students and that will be built to last for a long and sustainable future. Currently, Prekindergarten and Kindergarten classrooms have a class set of iPads to utilize in student small group work. Additionally, 8th grade students are each given an individual iPad to use at school and home during the school year. All grade levels will have access to iPad and laptop carts to use in the classrooms.

SmartBoards and mounted projectors also enhance the technological opportunities in the classrooms. The Learning Commons provides an area for students to access digital information. Students begin to focus on learning to type in 3rd grade. When students begin Middle School, they are given school email accounts and learn how to utilize Google Docs to manage their schoolwork.

Extracurricular Activities
The School offers extended time for students to stay after school for study and play. Students may remain at the school until 6 p.m. Lower School students may participate

in after school clubs, including Art, Spanish, Choir and Odyssey of the Mind. Middle School students may participate in after school athletics or additional extracurricular activities such as Choir, National Junior Honor Society and Odyssey of the Mind.

Athletics

Presbyterian School has an outdoor education campus away from the main campus with three rock-climbing walls and two gymnasiums. The 14-acre outdoor education campus, located less than 5 miles from the school, also has a pavilion, two athletic fields, an eight-lane track, an outdoor chapel, and a cross country trail. Students may participate in school-sponsored sports in sixth through eighth grade. Girls may join volleyball, cross country, or field hockey in the fall; soccer, swimming, or basketball in the winter; and golf, lacrosse, or track and field in the spring. Boys may join cross country, or football in the fall; basketball, soccer, or swimming in the winter; and golf, lacrosse, or track and field in the spring.

Presbyterian School of Houston Fast Facts

Overview

School Type	Religious, Coeducational
Religious Affiliation	Presbyterian
Date Founded	1988
Endowment	N/A
Grades Served	3 years old – 8th grade
Enrollment	512
Grade 8	53
Grade 7	60
Grade 6	60
Grade 5	49
Grade 4	43
Grade 3	41
Grade 2	40
Grade 1	38
Kindergarten	42
Pre-Kindergarten	86
Student to Teacher Ratio	8:1
Faculty with Advanced Degrees	N/A
Minorities in Student Body	12%

Curriculum

Academic Tracks Offered	On-Track
Languages Offered	Spanish
Calendar (Semester / Trimester / Other)	Trimester/Quarter
Interscholastic Sports Programs	10

Admissions

Prime Entry Points	3 years old, 6th grade
Pre-K	$14,260
Kindergarten	$15,700
Grades 1 - 4	$16,375
Grades 5 - 8	$18,770
New Student Fee	$500
Food Service	$1000
Students on Financial Aid	10%-15%

River Oaks Baptist School

2300 Willowick Road, Houston, TX 77027
713-623-6938
www.robs.org

Dr. Nancy Hightower, Head of School
Ms. Kristin Poe, Director of Admissions

Overview

In 1955, the River Oaks Baptist Church established the River Oaks Baptist School as a weekly preschool and kindergarten program with two teachers and thirty students. River Oaks Baptist gradually expanded to include the Lower School (elementary) and the Middle School (sixth through eighth grade) and graduated its first eighth grade class in 1979. By 1980, River Oaks Baptist grew to 527 students and began a master plan to enlarge the size of the campus and facilities. As of 2006, River Oaks Baptist can accommodate 870 students. The school remains at its original location next to River Oaks Baptist Church.

Religious Affiliation

While River Oaks Baptist was founded by the church, the student body is a mixture of religious backgrounds including Methodist, Presbyterian, Catholic, Episcopalian, and even those whose faith is not Christian. River Oaks Baptist incorporates the Christian faith into its curriculum, requiring students to attend weekly chapel services, morning devotionals, Bible classes, and community service projects. Lower School students have readings and discussions in homeroom, and Middle School students discuss spirituality in real-life situations during their group advisory class.

Location and Facilities

River Oaks Baptist is located in the River Oaks area, just north of Westheimer at 2300 Willowick Road. The surrounding neighborhood is residential and the campus includes a 9,000 square foot library and media center, a gymnasium with an indoor basketball court, and a full-sized track encompassing a soccer field. Large portions of the current school facilities were constructed after 1980. However, most of the buildings were renovated during a major construction campaign that began in 1996 and was completed in 2007. Currently, no future construction plans have been announced.

Admissions

River Oaks Baptist admission process requires 1) a completed application; 2) parents must attend either a school tour or open house; 3) register for group testing for ages 3 through fifth grade; 4) schedule an individual evaluation for Kindergarten through fourth grade; 5) ISEE and OLSAT results for fifth through eighth grade; 6) Parent Interview for fifth through eighth grade; 7) and Student Interview for sixth through eighth grade. Depending on the grade, group testing can include participating in a class and taking a reading and mathematics assessment test.

River Oaks Baptist does give weight to applicants whose parents or siblings have attended or currently attend the school. Students whose parents are members of the church or are current faculty/staff are also given preference in admission. Twenty percent of openings in age 2 (Discovery) through eighth grade will be reserved for applicants who have never attended the school nor have parents or siblings that have attended the school. Legacy does not guarantee a position at River Oaks Baptist.

Academic Tracks and Curriculum

River Oaks Baptist features On-Track and Honors curriculums, with the Honors curriculum beginning in seventh grade. In each grade, students complete a full year of English, science, math, history, and physical education. Fifth and sixth grade students complete seven-week rotations in Bible, art, music, theater arts, and computer. Seventh and eighth grade students must take four weeks of Bible each semester and must choose one of the following classes for each semester: art, music, theater arts, or computer. River Oaks Baptist hosts a two year Algebra I curriculum beginning in seventh grade. Honors courses include Algebra I, English, and Spanish 2.

Special Needs
No information provided.

Foreign Languages
River Oaks Baptist's Spanish Language curriculum begins with Discovery (age 2) students. Teachers expose the students to vocabulary through class discussions and software for Discovery through Pre-Kindergarten students. Previously learned science and math concepts are used a point of reference for further instruction in Spanish for Kindergarten through fourth grade students. Fifth grade students are taught almost entirely in Spanish for 30 minutes four times each week, while teachers continue to incorporate math and science concepts learned in English. Students in sixth through eighth grade may choose to follow the path of Spanish 1A6 in sixth grade, Spanish 1B7 in seventh grade, and Spanish 2 Honors in eighth grade. Students may opt out of Spanish their seventh and eighth grade year by taking an English Seminar where students study current young adult literature, such as *Unwind* and *The Hunger Games*.

Arts
River Oaks Baptists incorporates Fine Arts into its curriculum for all grades and includes music, art, and theater arts. Students play instruments and can perform in public venues. In art, students are exposed to weaving, printmaking, sculpting, and painting. Beginning in fifth grade, students have the opportunity to learn the fundamentals of theater arts and perform plays in seventh and eighth grade.

Technology
Classrooms are equipped with Smart Boards, overhead, LCD, and Document projectors. Students also have access to 14 desktop computers and 23 laptops.

Extracurricular Activities
River Oaks Baptist offers several after-school programs for its students. "Prime Time" is designed for students to complete homework after school until 6:00 PM. Students may also participate in after-school enrichment programs such as Chess, Chinese, Building Brains, Art, Dance, Drama/Musical Theater, Golf, Gymnastics, Mannerific, and Tae Kwon Do.

Athletics
Outside of physical education, River Oaks Baptist offers sports opportunities for its students as early as sixth grade. In sixth grade, boys and girls can participate in cross-country and track. In seventh and eighth grade, boys and girls may participate in volleyball, soccer, lacrosse, tennis, track and field, basketball, and cross country. Girls may also play in field hockey and softball, while boys may also play football. Kindergarten through sixth grade students can participate in the United Church Athletic League in baseball (K – 5th), basketball (2nd – 5th), soccer (K – 6th), and volleyball for girls (4th – 6th).

River Oaks Baptist School Fast Facts

Overview

School Type	Religious, Co-Educational
Religious Affiliation	Baptist
Date Founded	1955
Endowment	N/A
Grades Served	Age 2 – 8th
Enrollment	789
Grade 8	75
Grade 7	78
Grade 6	84
Grade 5	85
Grade 4	80
Grade 3	83
Grade 2	80
Grade 1	84
Kindergarten	83
Pre-Kindergarten	57
Student to Teacher Ratio	15:1
Faculty with Advanced Degrees (# / %)	# / 35.5%
Minorities in Student Body	N/A

Curriculum

Academic Tracks Offered	On-Track, Honors
Advanced Placement Courses Offered	N/A
Languages Offered	Spanish
Calendar (Semester / Trimester / Other)	Semester
Interscholastic Sports Programs	10

Admissions

Prime Entry Points	Discovery, Readiness, K, 6
Discovery (Age 2)	$7,445
Readiness (Age 3) and Pre-K	$13,730
Kindergarten	$15,540
Grades 1-4	$15,915
Grades 5-6	$17,625
Grades 7-8	$19,820
Student Fee	$200-$500
New Student Fee	$500
Lunch Fee Lower School	$675
Lunch Fee Middle School	$750
Prime Time	$2,600-$2,900
Students on Financial Aid	N/A

School of the Woods

1321 Wirt Road, Houston, TX 77055
713-686-8811
www.schoolofthewoods.org

Ms. Sherry Herron, Head of School
Ms. Sara Sornson, Director of Admissions

Overview

The School of the Woods was originally founded as a nursery school in 1962, a few years after Montessori education resurfaced in the United States. The school received its name to honor the work of Dr. Ernest and Hilda Wood in developing the school's curriculum. The School of the Woods formalized its commitment to the Montessori Method of education in 1973 by associating with the American Montessori Society. In 2002, the school added a twelfth grade. In that same year, the school received accreditation from the American Montessori Society, the Texas Alliance of Accredited Private Schools, and the Southern Association of Colleges and Schools.

Religious Affiliation

School of the Woods does not have any religious affiliation.

Location and Facilities

A student's environment is an important factor in the Montessori Method of education and the School of the Woods' location reflects this part of the school's curriculum. The school's 5-acre campus is located in a wooded area of Spring Branch, just one mile north of I-10. Texas Parks and Wildlife designated the campus's grounds a Wildlife Habitat in 2003 and the school buildings are designed after cottages.

Each classroom is fashioned after the Montessori method to be orderly and accessible to the age group, with natural light and Montessori materials. In the summer of 2002, the School of the Woods purchased a second 5-acre plot of land as the future site for a new high school at the corner of Wirt and Westview; development of this campus is on going. School of the Woods does not have any on-site athletic facilities. The school's teams compete at Memorial High School and have access to the gym at neighboring Holy Cross Lutheran Church.

Admissions

The School of the Woods features a rolling enrollment program, with all prospective students placed in a waiting pool. The school determines re-enrollment for its current students in February and notifies the parents of students in the waiting pool by April 1st whether or not their student has placed. Students may also be placed throughout the year if vacancies occur. Students are required to submit academic records from the last two years for applications to elementary to high school. Students applying to grades 9 through 11 must submit teacher recommendations, a photo of the student, a completed student questionnaire, and their ISEE score results. The student and his/her family will also participate in an interview.

Academic Tracks and Curriculum

Since the School of the Woods' inception in 1962, the school has followed the principals of Dr. Montessori, an Italian physician and educator (1870-1952). The Montessori Method emphasizes the natural development of the student with the teacher acting as a guide and not as an instructor. Each classroom is open and orderly and is filled with Montessori materials, such as the pink tower of blocks. Students are allowed to develop at their own pace, but within the specific limits of the classroom environment. From ages 2 ½ to 12 years, students participate in mixed age classrooms, where older students support younger students.

Instead of the traditional grading system, the School of the Woods implements a mastery learning system, which requires a student to master the current lesson with a very high accuracy rate before moving onto the next lesson. The upper school integrates the Montessori Method and the Texas requirements of essential elements where students must earn more than 24 credits to receive a high school diploma: English (4), Math (4), Science (3), Social Science (4), Foreign Language (2), Health (2), Technology (1.5), Fine Arts (1), Academic Electives (1), Speech (2), Computer Technology (2), Community Outreach (1), Career Education (1), Other Electives (.5).

Special Needs
The majority of the student population at School of the Woods has a diagnosed learning difference. As such, accommodating the unique needs of these students is an integral part of the school's curriculum and environment. All high school students have direct access to the principal, who serves as their counselor.

Foreign Languages
Students may take Spanish, French, or American Sign Language. Spanish is offered up to level five, while French and ASL are up to level four.

Arts
Students may participate in before and/or after school programs in addition to the school's curriculum. During the school day, students can choose between art classes such as painting and drawing, industrial design, and photography. Students may also participate in drama, gymnastics, and dance. The school offers after school music instruction for an additional fee in African drums, guitar, piano, and harp.

Technology
Students must bring a laptop to school with them. The school recommends a Mac since the technology department employs a Mac specialist; however, students may choose whatever computer they wish. There are strict usage parameters that students must obey while using their laptops during the school day.

Extracurricular Activities
The school's student council is called the "Orchestrators," and they are responsible for hosting events such as Prom and Homecoming. Other school-sponsored activities include speech and debate and philosophy. In general, students may start any club that they desire so long as they gain the school's approval.

Athletics
The school fields interscholastic teams in four sports: baseball, swimming, track, and volleyball.

School of the Woods Fast Facts

Overview

School Type	Montessori, Coeducational
Religious Affiliation	Nonsectarian
Date Founded	1962
Endowment	N/A
Grades Served	PreK-12
Enrollment	378
Grade 12	21
Grade 11	21
Grade 10	21
Grade 9	21
Grade 8	25
Grade 7	17
Grade 6	24
Grade 5	18
Grade 4	23
Grade 3	32
Grade 2	25
Grade 1	27
Kindergarten	38
Pre-Kindergarten	65
Student to Teacher Ratio	8:1
Faculty with Advanced Degrees (# / %)	N/A
Minorities in Student Body	22%

Curriculum

Academic Tracks Offered	Montessori
Advanced Placement Courses Offered	N/A
Languages Offered	Spanish, American Sign Language, French
Calendar (Semester / Trimester / Other)	Semester
Interscholastic Sports Programs	4

Graduating Seniors

National Merit Semi-Finalists (# / %)	0
Average SAT Scores	N/A
Mathematics	N/A
Critical Reading	N/A
Writing	N/A
% Students Admitted to 4 Year University	N/A

Admissions

Prime Entry Points	Age 2 ½, Age 6, Age 9, Age 12
Ages 2 ½ to 6	$5,694- $14,340
Ages 6 to 9	$10,935
Ages 9 to 12	$11,124
Ages 12 to 14	$13,446
Ages 14 to 18	$15,948
Full-Day Fee	$2,322
Off-campus field studies	$800-2,500
Facilities Fee	$550
Students on Financial Aid	N/A

Second Baptist School

6410 Woodway Dr, Houston, TX 77057   Dr. Jeff Williams, Head of School
713-365-2310   Andrea Prothro, Director of Admissions
www.SecondBaptistSchool.org

Overview

Second Baptist School (SBS) was founded in 1946 through Second Baptist Church. Located in what is now Midtown Houston, it welcomed its first class of 14 kindergarten students in 1947. By 1955, the school had expanded to a full elementary school with the addition of a sixth grade. In 1957, the school moved to its current location in the Memorial area of Houston and embarked on a steady expansion—opening a Middle School in 1974 and an Upper School in 1982. Today, the school educates more than 1,100 pre-kindergarteners through 12th grade seniors.

Religious Affiliation

The school is a "self-supporting ministry" of the Second Baptist Church of Houston. As such, members of Second Baptist Church receive discounts on tuition. Lower school students attend chapel once a week where they pledge to the American and Christian flags and the Bible. Middle School students attend a contemporary chapel service once a week. Upper School students are required to take Bible studies classes each year. Student "Professions of Faith" are encouraged and publicized.

Location and Facilities

SBS is located adjacent to Second Baptist Church on a 42-acre campus replete with nearly 1 million square feet of buildings. It is located in the Memorial area of Houston just south of the exclusive Houston Country Club and Racquet Club. It is fairly equidistant between Beltway 8, Loop 610, I-10, and the Westpark Tollway.

Admissions

The admissions process for middle and high school students includes six steps: 1) online application 2) family application 3) academic information - teacher recommendations and grades 4) standardized testing 5) and interviews. Additionally for upper school students there is also the opportunity for applicants to shadow a currently enrolled student.

Required tests for Pre-K through 4th grade include the WPPSI (or WISC for K-4) and a group evaluation. Additionally, applicants in grades 1-4 must also complete the Woodcock-Johnson Tests of Cognitive Abilities.

Applicants for grades 5-12 must take the ISEE test appropriate to the grade for which they are applying.

Academic Tracks and Curriculum

The Lower School curriculum is self-contained meaning that students stay in one room while the same group of teachers covers all of the subjects in the curriculum. The Middle and Upper Schools are departmentalized. Academic track differentiation begins in 7th grade when students have different math class options. Honors classes are offered beginning in the 9th grade. SBS offers 16 honors classes and 15 AP classes in the Upper School.

Interim Term is a two-week period in March, which gives students the opportunity to pursue interests outside of a standard school curriculum such as domestic and foreign travel, community service, cultural programs, and internships.

The school requires 23 credit hours to graduate; one credit is equivalent to one year of study: English (4), Math (3), Social Studies (3.5), Science (3), Foreign Languages (2),

Fine Arts (1), Economics (.5), Computer (1), Communication App. (.5), Electives (2.5), Physical Education (1.5). Bible instruction is required each year.

Special Needs
No information provided.

Foreign Languages
SBS provides instruction in French and Spanish. Foreign language instruction is offered beginning with kindergarten Spanish (but is discontinued from 1st through 5th grade). Spanish is offered continuously beginning in sixth grade through Advanced Placement Spanish Language. French is offered beginning in 9th grade. Students may study up to AP French Language.

Arts
Music and art instruction begin in Pre-Kindergarten where students benefit from weekly instruction. In addition to visual art in Middle School, students also have the option of band choir, acting, and drama. The Upper School arts department offers seventeen classes including AP Studio Art (Drawing, 2D Design, 3D Design). Photography is also available. In music, students can participate in choir, band, marching band, string ensemble, and music theory.

Technology
In the Lower School, weekly computer instruction begins in Kindergarten. As of 2011, students in 5th through 12th grade benefit from the school's "one-to-one" MacBook program. SBS owns the computers and provides students with new computers every three years. Students are not allowed to bring their own laptops to school even if it is a MacBook. Since the school owns the computers, there is no additional charge outside of existing tuition fees.

Extracurricular Activities
In the Middle and Upper Schools, the student council is comprised of class and school wide representatives. Mathematically inclined middle school students can join the math club. There are a number of other clubs ranging from academic team to debate to key club to language clubs and Model U.N. Qualifying students may participate in the National Honor Society and French, Latin, and Spanish language honor societies.

Athletics
Athletic facilities include three gymnasiums, weight room, locker rooms, and multipurpose fields: baseball field, softball field, football, and soccer field. The school fields teams across eleven sports: baseball, basketball, cheerleading, cross-country, football, golf, soccer, softball, tennis, track, and volleyball. SBS is a member of the Texas Association of Private and Parochial Schools (TAPPS).

Second Baptist School Fast Facts

Overview

School Type	Religious, Coeducational
Religious Affiliation	Baptist
Date Founded	1946
Endowment	N/A
Grades Served	Pre-K - 12
Enrollment	1,122
Grade 12	66
Grade 11	72
Grade 10	71
Grade 9	114
Grade 8	74
Grade 7	99
Grade 6	98
Grade 5	80
Grade 4	69
Grade 3	99
Grade 2	80
Grade 1	72
Kindergarten	78
Pre-Kindergarten	50
Student to Teacher Ratio	9/1
Faculty with Advanced Degrees (# / %)	58/ 34%
Minorities in Student Body	N/A

Curriculum

Academic Tracks Offered	On-Track, Honors, AP
Advanced Placement Courses Offered	15
Languages Offered	French, Spanish
Calendar (Semester / Trimester / Other)	Semester
Interscholastic Sports Programs	11

Graduating Seniors

National Merit Semi-Finalists (# / %)	2/3%
Average SAT Scores (Class of 2009)	1781
Mathematics	601
Critical Reading	583
Writing	597
% Students Admitted to 4 Year University	100

Admissions

Prime Entry Points	K, 1, 6, 9
Pre-Kindergarten	$8,772
Kindergarten – Grade 2	$12,168
Grades 3-4	$13,032
Grades 5-8	$15,120
Grades 9-12	$16,584
New Student Fee (PreK-4 / 5-12)	$300 / $400
Students on Financial Aid	N/A

St. Agnes Academy

9000 Bellaire Blvd., Houston, TX 77036
713-219-5499
www.St-Agnes.org

Sister Jane Meyer, Head of School
Ms. Brigid Schiro, Director of Admissions

Overview

The Prioress of the Dominican Sisters of Houston, Mother Pauline Gannon, founded St. Agnes Academy in 1905 and welcomed its first students in 1906. Originally located in modern day, midtown Houston, the school relocated to its current location in Sharpstown in 1963. St. Agnes originally provided 12 years of education and boarding facilities. It discontinued the boarding facilities in 1939 and converted to a high school in 1954.

Religious Affiliation

The Dominican Sisters of Houston administers St. Agnes. A Catholic religious order, the Dominicans date back to the Middle Ages, when Saint Dominic formed the order in the thirteenth century. The Dominican traditional pillars of prayer, study, community, and preaching are the core values of St. Agnes Academy. Prayer is held daily in first period class; Mass and confession are offered on Tuesdays during lunch.

Location and Facilities

St. Agnes's 15.6-acre campus is located in the Greater Sharptstown area of southwest Houston. It is fairly equidistant between the Sam Houston Tollway, Westpark Tollway, and Highway 59. Its campus is adjacent to brother school Strake Jesuit off of Bellaire Boulevard, the main street of Houston's sprawling Chinatown. The school's adjacent location to Strake allows the two schools to cooperate closely including sharing of facilities and some course offerings.

The school's dense campus is comprised of interconnected buildings centered on either the library or the courtyard. The science building and student life center was completed in 2007 and is instantly recognizable for its modern glass rotunda. Dedicated athletic facilities include a gym with two basketball courts and a softball field that overlaps with the soccer field. The school plans to vastly expand its athletic facilities on a nearby 18.7-acre space, which will include three playing fields, softball field, tennis courts and a track. It will also include a field house, concession stand and meetings rooms. In the meantime, other facilities, such as the pool and track are shared with Strake Jesuit.

Admissions

The school states that students admitted to St. Agnes in recent years have earned above average grades and scores on standardized tests. To this extent, the school cites the following criteria for admission—grades (6, 7, 8th grades), entrance exam scores (ISEE or HSPT), English and math teacher recommendations, student application and essay, attendance and discipline records, and work habits. The school administers the ISEE, but students applying to other Catholic high schools may also submit HSPT scores in lieu of the ISEE results.

Academic Tracks and Curriculum

Students at St. Agnes can enroll in classes across two tracks – college preparatory and Honors/Advance Placement. Honors classes are available from the freshman year. 12 AP classes are offered. Math offerings include AP Calculus AB and BC, statistics, and visual basic programming. Science courses include AP Biology, AP Chemistry, honors physics, geology, aquatic science, and astronomy. History and social science offerings include AP World History, AP US History, AP Government and microeconomics, psychology, Introduction to Law, Introduction to African American Studies, and even "The 1960's."

Twenty-six credits are required to graduate from St. Agnes; students must take a minimum of six credits per year: English (4), Theology (4), Mathematics (4), Science (4), Social Studies (3), Foreign Language (2), Fine Arts (1), PE/ Health (2), Community Service (.5), Communications (.5).

Special Needs
St. Agnes Academy's Academic Services Center, under direction of the Coordinator, is a place for students with various learning differences to attain skills in study techniques, time management, organizational strategies and goal planning, as well as providing accommodations for students to ensure their full participation in the academic programs. The Center is also a source for all students to develop effective learning and academic strategies to help meet the curriculum demands of St. Agnes Academy.

Foreign Languages
Students at St. Agnes are required to take two years of a foreign language to graduate. They may choose from French, Latin, Spanish or Chinese Mandarin. Spanish, French, and Latin are offered up to level 5. An AP class is offered for Spanish. Chinese is a new offering that began in the 2011 academic year and is a co-enrollment with Strake Jesuit.

Arts
St. Agnes requires only two semesters of fine arts. However, it does offer more than 25 options to its students across three departments – Fine Arts, Performing Arts, and Music. Fine arts courses include advanced study in drawing, studio art, photography/ video, and painting. Performing Arts offerings include cinema, acting, and stage production. Music electives include vocal performance, choir, and music theory. Band classes are available through Strake Jesuit.

Technology
The school's laptop program requires that all incoming students purchase a Windows based tablet computer that is heavily integrated into the curriculum. The school selects the computer each year; Students do not have a choice of computer or vendor. In addition to the laptop program, students may also take a handful of business and computer education courses. Offerings include accounting, web mastering, and computer applications.

Extracurricular Activities
St. Agnes supports a wide variety of extra-curricular and co-curricular activities. Music examples include choir, band, and private voice lessons. Drama options include roles at plays and musicals performed not only at St. Agnes but also at Strake Jesuit and St. Thomas. Campus publications include a newspaper, online blog, literary magazine, and yearbook. Students may also try out for cheerleading squads at Strake Jesuit and St. Thomas or join the school's own dance team.

The Student Council includes elected representatives as well as an appointed representative from each grade. Representatives are divided into four committees— drugs and alcohol, safety and health, pride and patriotism, and energy and the environment. The Campus Ministry Team is also a large student organization which helps plan the annual, mandatory class retreats, assists with liturgies, and participates in community service.

Athletics
All sports are offered at the junior varsity and varsity level with the exception of golf. Freshman only teams are fielded in volleyball and basketball. Water polo, lacrosse, and field hockey are run by organizations independent from St. Agnes. St. Agnes

currently uses the track and pools facilities at Strake Jesuit; however the completion of the new athletic facilities will allow St. Agnes to move all sports to the new location with the exception of basketball, volleyball, swimming and golf. The school fields teams across twelve sport: basketball, cross-country, field hockey, golf, lacrosse, soccer, swimming, softball, tennis, track, water polo, and volleyball. St. Agnes is a member of the Texas Association of Private and Parochial (TAPPS) Schools.

St. Agnes Academy Fast Facts

Overview

School Type	Religious, Girls
Religious Affiliation	Catholic
Date Founded	1906
Endowment (reported on 7/31/10)	N/A
Grades Served	9-12
Enrollment	874
Grade 12	208
Grade 11	212
Grade 10	225
Grade 9	229
Student to Teacher Ratio	15:1
Faculty with Advanced Degrees (# / %)	>75%
Minorities in Student Body	35%

Curriculum

Academic Tracks Offered	College Prep, Honors, AP
Advanced Placement Courses Offered	12
Languages Offered	Chinese, French, Latin, Spanish
Calendar (Semester / Trimester / Other)	Semester
Interscholastic Sports Programs	12

Graduating Seniors

National Merit Semi-Finalists (# / %)	12/6%
Average SAT Scores (Class of 2011)	1905
Mathematics	640
Critical Reading	625
Writing	640
% Students Admitted to 4 Year University	99%

Admissions

Prime Entry Points	Grade 9
Grades 9-12	$14,550
Registration Fee	$100
Students on Financial Aid	10%

St. Catherine's Montessori

9821 Timberside, Houston, TX 77025
713-665-2195
www.StCathMont.org

Ms. Susan Tracy, Head of School
Ms. Laurie Farris, Director of Admissions

Overview

Sisters Edna Ann Herbert and Shirley Owens founded St. Catherine's Montessori (originally named Dominican Montessori) in 1966 and are affiliated with the Association Montessori Internationale. Before moving to its current location in 2006, St. Catherine's was hosted by St. Agnes Academy's old building. The Holy Rosary Parish and Bering Memorial Methodist Church then hosted the school. In 1983, St. Catherine's occupied a 20,000 square foot building on Westridge. St. Catherine's works with students age 14 months to ninth grade.

Religious Affiliation

St. Catherine's is part of the Catholic Diocese of Galveston-Houston and incorporates the Catholic faith with Dr. Montessori's educational system through the "Catechesis of the Good Shepherd." The school features an atrium where students gather and interact with spiritual objects as a sensorial experience of the Catholic faith. The school's spiritual goal for its students is "...to offer a pervasive element of Catholic study and experiences within the educational setting." St. Catherine's is also a member of the National Catholic Education Association.

Location and Facilities

St. Catherine's 7.4-acre campus is located near the 610 Loop and is between Stella Link and South Main. The school includes a gymnasium, sports field, and gardens. St. Catherine's is Leadership in Energy and Environmental Design (LEED) certified, which is the current rating system for the operation of "green" buildings. "Green" features of St. Catherine's include water use reduction, storm water management, energy from 100% renewable resources, use of recycled materials, construction waste management, and green housekeeping.

Admissions

In order to receive an application, parents must complete a tour (parents only) and classroom observation, in that order. Tours are generally scheduled on Tuesdays from 9:00 to 10:00 AM. Once the tour is completed, the classroom observation is scheduled, usually on Wednesdays from 9:00 to 10:00 AM. Applications are considered in February, giving greater priority to 1) siblings of current St. Catherine's students and 2) transfer students from other Montessori schools over other applicants.

Students coming from a non-Montessori background are eligible on a space available basis in first and fourth grade only. Applicants for seventh through ninth grade must be a transfer student from a Montessori school with at least three continuous years of experience. St. Catherine's also requires the student's most recent report cards, progress reports, and achievement test scores. The school will schedule a visit for the student and one of the school's guides will perform an informal evaluation.

Academic Tracks and Curriculum

St. Catherine's curriculum follows the educational methodology implemented by Dr. Maria Montessori in 1897. In accordance with Dr. Montessori's multi-age classrooms, the school groups its students together in threes: 14 months to age 3 (Toddler), age 4 to age 6 (Primary), first through third grade (Lower Elementary), fourth through sixth grade (Upper Elementary), and seventh through ninth grade (Adolescent Community). While the Montessori Method was designed for up to sixth grade students, St. Catherine's continues to employ the method and incorporates traditional American education elements in seventh through ninth grade. The Adolescent Community studies History and Civilization, Science, English/Language Arts, Mathematics, Theology, Physical Education, and Music.

Special Needs
No information provided.

Foreign Languages
For the Adolescent Community, St. Catherine's offers Spanish I, Spanish II, and Spanish for Native Speakers to its students.

Arts
Students attending St. Catherine's have the opportunity to study Liturgical Music and participate in the Upper School Musical Production. Students may also join the school's Band and Orchestra programs and join Dance Class.

Technology
No information provided.

Extracurricular Activities
St. Catherine's offers a number of after school activities for Primary students and up. Primary students may participate in Construction Camp and Natural Wonders. Elementary students may join Junkyard Wars Junior and Super Science Sleuths. Primary students and older may participate in Gymnastics.

Athletics
St. Catherine's hosts after-school athletics programs for Primary through Adolescent Community students. Students may participate in soccer, volleyball, basketball, and track and field.

St. Catherine's Montessori Fast Facts

Overview

School Type	Religious, Montessori, Coeducational
Religious Affiliation	Catholic
Date Founded	1966
Endowment	N/A
Grades Served	Age 14 mo. – 9th
Enrollment	155
Grade 9	5
Grade 8	10
Grade 7	16
Grade 6	14
Grade 5	14
Grade 4	14
Grade 3	13
Grade 2	22
Grade 1	21
Kindergarten	26
Pre-Kindergarten	85
Student to Teacher Ratio	10:1
Faculty with Advanced Degrees (# / %)	N/A
Minorities in Student Body	52%

Curriculum

Academic Tracks Offered	Montessori
Advanced Placement Courses Offered	N/A
Languages Offered	Spanish
Calendar (Semester / Trimester / Other)	Semester
Interscholastic Sports Programs	4

Admissions

Prime Entry Points	Toddler, 1st Grade, 4th Grade
Toddler	$7,694
Primary (full day)	$9,186
Elementary (grade 1 – 6)	$9,960
Adolescent Community (grade 7 – 9)	$10,720
New Student Fee	$450
Tuition Deposit	$750
Upper Elementary Fees	$775
Adolescent Community Fees	$1,950
Students on Financial Aid	N/A

St. Francis Episcopal Day School

355 Piney Point Rd, Houston, TX 77024   Ms. Susan Lair, Head of School
713-458-6100   Ms. Margaret Ann Casseb, Head of Admissions
www.sfedshouston.org

Overview

Founded in 1952 as a mission of St. Francis Episcopal Church, St. Francis Episcopal started with a class of 24 kindergarteners. Still residing at its original location, near the church, St. Francis now serves grades Pre-K through 8th grade. The school cites four cornerstones that guide its offerings: faith, scholarship, courage, and honor.

Religious Affiliation

St. Francis Episcopal educates students in the Anglican tradition. However, the school not only accepts students of all faiths, but also states that religious pluralism is one of its central goals. Religious education at St. Francis takes the form of community service projects and biweekly services.

Location and Facilities

St. Francis Episcopal is situated on 15.5 wooded acres at 335 Piney Point Road in a residential area near Memorial. St. Francis's campus includes a Fine Arts center that seats 600, a 7,000 square foot library and technology center, and an outdoor nature-exploration classroom. Athletic facilities include a gymnasium and four acres of athletic fields that include two baseball diamonds, as well as soccer and lacrosse fields. Most of the school buildings were built between 1978 and 1985. In 2001, the school constructed a new Lower School building, library, Fine Arts Center, and technology center. The dining hall, gym, and other facilities were renovated as part of this campaign.

Admissions

For pre-primary students (18-39 months), parents must fill out an application. For primary students, parents must fill out an application and schedule an observation session. If the child has attended another school, then the parents must also submit a teacher recommendation. Kindergarten and 1st grade students must submit an application, a teacher recommendation, and WPPSI/WISC test scores and schedule an observation session. 2nd-4th graders must submit an application, a teacher recommendation, a transcript, OLSAT scores, and schedule a school visit.

For middle school (5th-8th grade) admissions, students must submit an application, OLSAT and ISEE scores, recommendations from their math and English teachers, transcripts, and schedule a visit during school hours. Parents may also schedule a visit for themselves. An interview and an all day visit during the school day are required. The school looks for students who are "a good fit for our culture, community and mission statement" and accepts students whose abilities "range from average to exceptional."

Legacy is a factor in admission, with the following order of preference: 1) qualified children of St. Francis church members, 2) qualified siblings of students continuing in the school, and 3) other qualified candidates.

Academic Tracks and Curriculum

St. Francis offers two tracks, On Track and Honors Pre-AP (for English and math). Students can begin taking honors math in 5th grade and can begin honors English in 6th grade. Students are selected for the Honors Pre-AP program based on their standardized test scores, their in-house placement exam scores, teacher recommendations, and course grades. If the student does not maintain a B- average in the Honors Pre-AP program, the student will be removed from the program. Placement in the program is only guaranteed for one year. Each year, the student will be reassessed by the same criteria in order to continue in the program.

Special Needs

No information provided about accommodations for students with learning differences such as ADHD, dysgraphia, or processing disorders. However, each student is assigned a faculty advisor, and all students complete a Life Skills program.

Foreign Languages

St. Francis only offers Spanish as its foreign language. New students have the opportunity to participate in a Spanish tutorial program in August before school starts if needed.

Arts

Art courses offered include "Art a la Carte", Art History, Choral Music, Drama, Music History, Orchestra, Stage Tech, and Visual Art. The art courses are held on a rotating schedule, and St. Francis holds numerous special art events throughout the school year, including student studio art exhibitions, choir performances, orchestra performances, two main-stage theater productions, and one-act plays.

Technology

Students have access to four computer labs, one specifically containing iMacs and one specifically containing PCs, as well as laptop carts. Every classroom also contains a SMART Board. In 5th and 6th grade, students take computer literacy courses. Seventh graders attend a multimedia technology class, and eighth graders can take an elective yearbook class where they learn Adobe InDesign, as well as Photoshop and Illustrator.

Extracurricular Activities

The school provides multiple community service opportunities, and service projects are incorporated into the curriculum. Students have many leadership opportunities through participation in Councils – Athletics Council, Chapel Council, Fine Arts Council, Student Council, etc. Students can also join the National Junior Honor Society.

Athletics

All students may sign up for three sports each year, one each in the fall, winter, and spring. All-boys teams include football, wrestling, soccer, basketball, and lacrosse, while all-girls teams include field hockey, volleyball, soccer, basketball, softball, and lacrosse. Co-ed sports include cross-country and track and field

St. Francis Episcopal Fast Facts

Overview

School Type	Religious, Coeducational
Religious Affiliation	Episcopal
Date Founded	1952
Endowment	N/A
Grades Served	PreK-8
Enrollment	645
Grade 8	71
Grade 7	86
Grade 6	84
Grade 5	83
Grade 4	52
Grade 3	72
Grade 2	56
Grade 1	65
Kindergarten	76
Pre-Kindergarten	175
Student to Teacher Ratio	7:1
Faculty with Advanced Degrees (# / %)	N/A
Minorities in Student Body	20%

Curriculum

Academic Tracks Offered	On Track, Honors Pre-AP
AP Courses	N/A
Languages Offered	Spanish
Calendar (Semester / Trimester / Other)	Quarter
Interscholastic Sports Programs	10

Admissions

Prime Entry Points	Pre-K, K, 5
Pre-K	$5,550-$16,750
Kindergarten- Grade 4	$16,750
Grades 5-8	$19,960
New Student Fee	$500
Students on Financial Aid	N/A

St. John's School

2401 Claremont Lane, Houston, TX 77019
713-850-0222
www.SJS.org

Dr. Mark Desjardins, Headmaster
Ms. Cheryl Plummer, Director of Admissions

Overview

At the behest of members of the Houston community, St. John's School was founded in 1946 in coordination with the Episcopal Church of St. John the Divine. A former Assistant Dean of Students at the University of Chicago, Alan Lake Chidsey served as the school's first headmaster when he welcomed 344 students to the school in its inaugural year. St. John's School is no longer formally affiliated with the church.

Religious Affiliation

Originally a joint effort with the Episcopal Church of St. John's the Divine, St. John's is today not religiously affiliated. The chapel on campus is host to a broad range of multicultural services in addition to non-denominational Judeo-Christian services.

Location and Facilities

St. John's 28-acre campus is located in the Upper Kirby district at the edge of Houston's affluent River Oaks community at the intersection of Westheimer Road and Buffalo Speedway. Westheimer Road divides it in the center. The Upper and Middle Schools are on the north side while the Lower School is on the south side of Westheimer. Two tunnels underneath Westheimer provide a traffic-free connection between the two halves of campus. Lamar High School is located across the street. Athletic facilities include a track and field, another multipurpose field, and a soccer/baseball field.

Admissions

The admissions process to St. John's is very competitive. Only about 20% of applicants are given offers of admission. Admissions criteria include academic capability, personal motivation, comparative strengths, and diversity. St. John's makes a conscious effort to admit students from all ethnic and socio-economic backgrounds. The school strongly favors community members or those who have some sort of affiliation with the school—alumni, siblings, faculty members, etc. Prospective parents would be well served by reading St. John's detailed publication on the admissions process, "Hopes and Realities," available on the school's website.

Kindergarten students must be 5 years old by September 1st but not older than 6 on June 1st of their application year. Only 175 candidates are allowed to apply for kindergarten. Preference is given to families affiliated with the school followed by chronological order of application date. There are 42 openings; historically, nearly 75% of these openings have been taken by legacy children. Applying students are individually administered IQ tests and also assessed in a group setting for school readiness skills.

Approximately 22 spaces are made available for first grade. Applicants should be six years old by September 1st but no older than 7 on June 1st. The evaluation process includes a teacher recommendation, testers' evaluations, IQ test, math achievement test, and writing sample. Legacy students historically account for 40% of the first grade openings.

The next prime entry point is sixth grade when approximately 50 spots are offered. Admissions criteria include teacher recommendations in math and English, mid-year report cards, test results from the OSLAT and ISEE, and an interview. Legacy students historically account for about 30% of sixth grade openings.

Ninth grade is the last prime entry point for St. John's with approximately 25 spaces offered. Application criteria include math and English teacher recommendations, mid-year report cards, OLSAT and ISEE test results, an essay, and an interview. Legacy students historically account for 40% of ninth grade openings.

Academic Tracks and Curriculum

The curriculum in kindergarten through third grade is self-contained meaning that students stay in one room while the same group of teachers covers all of the subjects in the curriculum. Subject specialists start teaching language arts, history, and math beginning in fourth grade. Art, computer, library, music, physical education, science, and Spanish are always taught by specialists regardless of grade.

The Middle School curriculum begins in sixth grade and is taught only by specialized teachers. Students participate in weekly enrichment courses including newspaper, student government, music, and sports. All students must participate in daily physical education.

In the Upper School, honors and advanced classes in math and English are generally offered beginning in eleventh grade. Over 17 Advanced Placement courses are offered. St. John's offers an advanced math curriculum including courses in linear algebra, partial differential equations, differential equations, and multivariable calculus. Juniors and seniors have access to a wide array of elective classes. Juniors and seniors may also participate in independent and directed study programs whereby they are able to create their own curricula. A pass / fail option is offered for elective classes.

The school requires 19.5 academic credits to earn a diploma; two semesters is equal to one credit: English (4), Math (3), Science (2), Foreign Language (3), Fine Arts (1), Electives (1.5), Physical Education (2).

Special Needs

No information provided.

Foreign Languages

Foreign language instruction is part of the St. John's curriculum beginning with compulsory Spanish in Kindergarten. French, Latin, and Spanish become available in sixth grade and are part of the curriculum four times a week. Chinese is offered beginning in 9th grade. French, Latin, and Spanish are offered up to and beyond the AP level.

Arts

An integral part of the Lower School curriculum, fine arts become more diversified beginning in sixth grade where all students must take one quarter each of theatre, dance, music, and art. A full year band class becomes optional in seventh grade. The options continue to expand in eighth grade and upper school.

Only one credit of art is required for graduation from St. John's; however, there are a wide variety of options for students to fulfill that credit including classes in photography, architecture, music theory, theatre, and even the history of rock and roll. Additionally, St. John's has a Performing Ensembles department, which includes Handbell, Jazz Band, String, Wind, Choir, and Dance Caprice. The Theatre department put on five major productions in the 2010-2011 academic year.

Technology

St. John's students begin visiting the computer lab in Kindergarten. Specialized computer classes start in the second grade and continue through middle school. Computer science becomes optional in the upper school with just three courses offered.

Wireless internet is available throughout the school's campus. Students are not required to bring their own laptops.

Extracurricular Activities
Students may participate in student government beginning in the Middle School. The Upper School publishes a monthly newspaper, *The Review*. It also publishes an annual magazine. Students can form just about any club they want if approved by the Dean of Students. Clubs are numerous and as diverse as the student body ranging from Model UN to Quiz Bowl to Spanish Club and the like.

Athletics
The school fields teams in fourteen sports: baseball, basketball, cross-country, field hockey, football, golf, lacrosse, soccer, swimming, softball, tennis, track, volleyball, and wrestling. St. John's is a member of the Southwest Preparatory Conference.

St. John's Fast Facts

Overview

School Type	Independent, Coeducational
Religious Affiliation	None
Date Founded	1946
Endowment	~$59M
Grades Served	K-12
Enrollment	1227
Grade 12	132
Grade 11	129
Grade 10	133
Grade 9	145
Grade 8	113
Grade 7	116
Grade 6	117
Grade 5	60
Grade 4	60
Grade 3	60
Grade 2	60
Grade 1	60
Kindergarten	42
Student to Teacher Ratio	7:1
Faculty with Advanced Degrees (# / %)	86/53%
Minorities in Student Body	19%

Curriculum

Academic Tracks Offered	On Track, Honors, AP
Advanced Placement Courses Offered	17
Languages Offered	Chinese, French, Latin, Spanish
Calendar (Semester / Trimester / Other)	Trimester
Interscholastic Sports Programs	14

Graduating Seniors

National Merit Semi-Finalists 2011(# / %)	46/35%
Average SAT Scores (Class of 2011)	2140
Mathematics	725
Critical Reading	700
Writing	715
% Students Admitted to 4 Year University	100%

Admissions

Prime Entry Points	K, 1, 6, 9
Kindergarten – Grade 5	$16,415
Grades 6-8	$19,100
Grades 9-12	$20,235
New Student Fee	$1000
Books and Supplies	$250-$1,200
Activity Fee	$110-$270
Athletics & Trips Fee	$50-$1,400
Students on Financial Aid	13%

St. Mark's Episcopal School

3816 Bellaire Boulevard, Houston, TX 77025   Mr. Garhett Wagers, Head of School
713-667-7030   Ms. Amanda Grace, Director of Admissions
www.STMES.org

Overview

St. Mark's Episcopal School celebrated its fiftieth anniversary in 2010. The school began as a nursery program for St. Mark's Episcopal Church in 1960. Over the next twenty years, St. Mark's expanded to serve students in grades K-8, graduating its first eighth grade class in 1988. Today, St. Mark's enrolls 396 students from ages two years through eighth grade. St. Mark's is accredited by the Southwest Association of Episcopal Schools.

Religious Affiliation

St. Mark's, a parish day school, follows the guidelines of the Episcopal Diocese of Texas. Students attend weekly chapel services and attend religion classes planned to support the growth of their personal faith, respect for others, and a sense of service. St. Mark's welcomes families of all faiths and encourages them to participate in the Episcopal rituals only so far as their faiths allow. The school honor code is founded on the principals of respect, responsibility, and kindness.

Location and Facilities

The school is located on the southwest edge of West University Place, a self-incorporated town within Houston's 610 Loop. An affluent neighborhood of single-family homes is directly to the school's north and east. Shopping centers are to its west and south. The campus includes four main buildings, which are home to classrooms, three computer labs, two libraries, two science labs, a gymnasium with stage, and a cafeteria. Buildings surround a courtyard, gardens, and two play grounds.

Admissions

St. Mark's seeks to "...enroll well-motivated children capable of academic challenge." Age requirements are as follows: Preschool 2's Program (2 by August 1), Preschool 3's Program (3 by August 1), Pre-Kindergarten and Kindergarten (4 or 5 respectively by August 1). The school grants priority consideration to members of St. Mark's Episcopal Church and siblings of currently enrolled children. Applications are accepted year round, but the deadline for priority enrollment is December 3, 2012.

Parents must fill out an application that includes a short answer question about their expectations for their child and includes their child's picture. Other required forms include a transcript request form, a teacher recommendation form for students in Early Childhood through Kindergarten, Grades 1-5, and two teacher recommendation forms (English and math) for students in Grades 6-8. For grades PK-8, St. Mark's requires an admissions test: the WPPSI-III (PK and K), WISC-IV (Grades 1-4) and the ISEE (Grades 5-8). Early Childhood applicants must attend a Saturday Group Observation in January or February; students applying for grades 1-8 must attend an in-school observation and/or interview with the school.

Academic Tracks and Curriculum

St. Mark's divides its student body into two divisions: the Lower School (Preschool 2s through Grade 4) and the Middle School (Grades 5-8). Curriculums in both divisions follow the school's core values of trustworthiness, respect, responsibility, fairness, and caring. The early childhood curriculum is designed to develop cognitive, social, emotional, creative, and fine and gross motor skills. The core curriculum for Grades 1-8 includes math, science, social studies and language arts. Service learning projects are planned for each grade level with school-wide initiatives lead by the Student Council.

The Upper Middle School (Grades 7 and 8) curriculum includes honors and Pre-AP classes.

Special Needs
St. Mark's accepts students with learning differences who have demonstrated their ability to succeed in a mainstream, traditional curriculum. The school is unable to serve children whose special educational needs require facilities and training surpassing the expertise of the faculty and staff. Students with learning differences are considered individually for admission to the school.

Foreign Languages
Spanish is introduced in the early years through stories and vocabulary exercises, with formal Spanish instruction beginning in the fourth grade. Fourth to sixth grade students are further exposed to Spanish through visual and performance activities. The Spanish program for seventh and eighth grade students follows a traditional format and is designed to prepare students for high school Spanish II.

Arts
The Lower and Middle School arts curriculum includes classes in studio art, music, and drama. Students in the preschool program attend music and movement classes. Students in grades K-4 have one semester of art and one of music, attending each class three times per week. Students in grades 5-8 have one quarter of art and one quarter of music each year. Additionally, elective classes for middle school students include dance, art, improvisation, podcasting & videography, speech, and yearbook.

Technology
Students are introduced to projects-based technology skills beginning in Pre-Kindergarten and continuing through eighth grade. The Lower School curriculum introduces keyboarding, graphic art tools, word processing and the creation of slideshows. The Middle School curriculum teaches technology skills as an integral part of the curriculum. Through quarterly classes, students learn Microsoft Office, basic web design, and film making.

Extracurricular Activities
Clubs meet Monday-Thursday from 3:30 to 4:30 during the fall and spring semesters. Clubs include chess, music lessons, robotics, cooking, sculpture, origami, fencing, and more. Student Council is also offered. Middle school students serve in advisory groups, which complete Service Learning projects together and are designed to develop relationships between the students. Service Learning projects take place throughout the year and include activities through The Diaper Foundation, Houston Food Bank, and Make-A-Wish Foundation. Elementary and middle school students may also participate in PSIA (Private School Interscholastic Association), which includes events such as Dictionary Skills, Spelling, Impromptu Speaking, Mathematics, Number Sense, and more.

Athletics
The school fields teams in grades 6-8 in six sports: boy's soccer, girl's volleyball, boys and girls basketball, track, golf and tennis. St. Mark's is a part of the Greater Houston Athletic Conference.

St. Mark's Episcopal School Fast Facts

Overview

School Type	Religious, Coeducational
Religious Affiliation	Episcopal
Date Founded	1960
Endowment	N/A
Grades Served	Two Years – 8th
Enrollment	396
Grade 8	38
Grade 7	32
Grade 6	28
Grade 5	27
Grade 4	32
Grade 3	32
Grade 2	32
Grade 1	40
Kindergarten	39
Pre-Kindergarten	94
Student to Teacher Ratio	14:1
Faculty with Advanced Degrees (# / %)	45%
Minorities in Student Body	30%

Curriculum

Academic Tracks Offered	On-Track, Honors, Pre-AP
Advanced Placement Courses Offered	N/A
Languages Offered	Spanish
Calendar (Semester / Trimester / Other)	Semester
Interscholastic Sports Programs	6

Admissions

Prime Entry Points	Two Years, Kindergarten, 6th Grade
Preschool 2's (full five days)	$9,088
Preschool 3's (full five days)	$10,386
Pre-Kindergarten	$13,874
Kindergarten	$14,010
Grades 1 – 4	$14,146
Grades 5 – 8	$15,748
New Student Fee	$495
Registration Fee	$595
Tuition Release Plan	$395
Students on Financial Aid	10%

St. Pius X High School

811 W. Donovan St., Houston, TX 77091   Sister Donna Pollard, O.P., President
713-692-3581   Ms. Susie Kramer, Director of Admissions
www.stpiusx.org

Overview
The Dominican Sisters, a Catholic women's group, founded St. Pius X High School in 1956 as part of Bishop Wendelin Nold's campaign to form new high schools in Houston. 50 years prior to St. Pius X's opening, the Dominican Sisters founded St. Agnes Academy, an all-girl's Catholic high school. St. Pius X is coeducational and also hosts a number of international students from over 20 different countries in its foreign exchange program.

Religious Affiliation
As the Dominican Sisters sponsor St. Pius X High School, the school follows the Four Pillars of the Dominican life, which develops the social, spiritual, intellectual, physical, and emotional aspects of a student. These pillars are:

- Prayer: members of the Dominican faith are encouraged to explore all methods of prayer, such as meditation, creative works, and the liturgy, in order to obtain a deeper awareness of God's presence.
- Study: through education, members of the Dominican faith discover and attempt to understand God's work in the contemporary world.
- Community: community service is an integral part of the Dominican faith. Its members establish and nurture relationships within the community and develop their spiritual selves in the process.
- Preaching: members preach their faith through living their lives, while a few are called to formally preach to the community.

Location and Facilities
St. Pius is located in the North Heights near the intersection of North Shepherd and West Tidwell Road. It is easily accessed off of I-45 and the 610 Loop. The campus is surrounded mostly by single-family homes on the North, West, and South. Commercial real estate is on the school's East side. The spacious, wooded campus features a football stadium and baseball/ softball fields.

Admissions
St. Pius X requires all applicants to complete the application form, which contains the Student Information Form (filled out by the parent) and the Student Inquiry Form (filled out by the student). The student must handwrite an essay about his/her short-term and long-term goals and why St. Pius X will satisfy those goals. Along with the application and essay, evaluation forms from the student's current principal/counselor, English teacher, and math teacher must also be submitted. Students are required to take the HSPT. Once all of the material has been submitted and deemed acceptable, students entering 9th grade and their parents will take part in an interview with St. Pius X faculty. Shadowing is available upon appointment.

Academic Tracks and Curriculum
St. Pius X features an Honors Track, which includes Advanced Placement courses, and a College Preparatory Track. Students are required to complete 4 credits of Theology, English, Mathematics, and Science, 3.5 credits in the Social Sciences, and 2 credits of a foreign language. The school offers Advanced Placement courses in English Literature, English Language, Government, Biology, Latin, Spanish, Computer Science, US History, Calculus AB, and Calculus BC. St. Pius X also offers students the option of three dual-credit courses, which are English IV, Psychology, and Government.

Students must earn 26 credits to graduate; one credit equals one year of study: English (4), Theology (4), Math (4), Science (4), Social Studies (4), Foreign Language/Reading Development (2), Physical Education (1.5), Fine Arts (1), Health (.5), Speech (.5), & Christian Service Learning (.5).

Special Needs

Upon submission of the application, St. Pius X reviews the student's information and determines if there is a need for accommodations. If there is a need, the application is sent to The Learning for Success Program. The parents are then given the option to apply to the program and submit the student's most recent psycho-educational evaluation. The Learning for Success Program Director reviews the application and determines whether or not the student will receive accommodations on the HSPT. Admittance to the program is based on entrance exam scores, the application and evaluation form, an interview, and recommendations.

Accommodations include academic strategy courses, in-class observation and support, after school tutorials, math and reading programs, extended time on tests, consultation and strategies for working with learning differences, and individualized accommodation plans. The Learning for Success Program is split into three tiers with varying degrees of support and accommodations: Tier 3 (no fee), Tier 2 ($1500), and Tier 1 ($2000, 9th to 10th grade only).

Foreign Languages

St. Pius X features foreign language courses in French, Italian, Spanish, and Latin, including Advanced Placement courses in Spanish and Latin. Students must take two years of the same language to satisfy graduation requirements.

Arts

St. Pius X hosts a variety of fine arts programs, such as band, choir, and theatre. Students can enroll in courses that will develop their skills in ceramics, painting, jewelry, and more. Students may choose to participate in Digital Photography, which teaches students how to take, edit, and print digital photographs. The school also offers a course in Graphic Design Techniques, where students will work with Adobe Photoshop CS4 and Adobe In Design CS4, and Jazz Band.

Technology

St. Pius has a Business and Computer Science Department, which offers Computer Science as one of its courses.

Extracurricular Activities

St. Pius X hosts a number of clubs and organizations in which students may participate. Students may join clubs such as Anime, Black History, Respect Life, and the Spanish Club. Students may also join societies such as International Thespians Society and the National Honors Society. Students interested in organizations that involve government may join the Student Council or the Student Cabinet, a group which acts as representatives of St. Pius X in events such as the Souper Bowl and Annual Baby Food Drive.

Athletics

St. Pius features nine sports programs for each gender in which its students can participate. Boys may join Baseball, Basketball, Cross Country, Football, Tennis, Track, Swimming, Ruby, and Golf. Girls may join Softball, Volleyball, Basketball, Cross Country, Golf, Soccer, Swimming, Tennis, and Track. Over half of St. Pius X's student body participates in its athletics programs at any given point. St. Pius X's athletic department also hosts a Booster Club in which two representatives from each sport are encouraged to participate.

St. Pius X Fast Facts

Overview

School Type	Religious, Coeducational
Religious Affiliation	Catholic
Date Founded	1956
Endowment	N/A
Grades Served	9-12
Enrollment	695
Grade 9	174
Grade 10	196
Grade 11	170
Grade 12	155
Student to Teacher Ratio	15:1
Faculty with Advanced Degrees (# / %)	N/A
Minorities in Student Body	51%

Curriculum

Academic Tracks Offered	College Preparatory, Honors/AP
Advanced Placement Courses Offered	10
Languages Offered	French, Italian, Spanish, Latin
Calendar (Semester / Trimester / Other)	Semester
Interscholastic Sports Programs	12

Graduating Seniors

National Merit Semi-Finalists (# / %)	1/0.6%
Average SAT Scores	N/A
Mathematics	N/A
Critical Reading	N/A
Writing	N/A
% Students Admitted to 4 Year University	N/A

Admissions

Prime Entry Points	9th grade
Grades 9-12	$11,700
Tier 1 Learning Center	$2,500
Tier 2 Learning Center	$2,000
New Student Fee	$300
Registration Fee	$200
Students on Financial Aid	N/A

St. Stephen's Episcopal School

1800 Sul Ross, Houston, TX 77098
713-821-9100
www.SSESH.org

Mr. David Coe, Head of School
Ms. Alycia Stewart, Director of Admissions

Overview
St. Stephen's was originally founded in 1971 as a parish school at Palmer Memorial Episcopal Church following the educational curriculum of Dr. Maria Montessori. The school moved to the St. Stephen's Episcopal Church facility in 1983 and was incorporated as St. Stephen's Episcopal School in 1987. The middle school was established in 1991 and the high school in 1998. St. Stephen's is accredited by the American Montessori Society and Southwestern Association of Episcopal Schools.

Religious Affiliation
St. Stephen's Episcopal is affiliated with the St. Stephen's Episcopal Church and students are required to attend chapel regularly. The school incorporates a Christian atmosphere within the Montessori Method of education, a program that is non-religious in nature. The school and the church host joint events and activities for the students attending St. Stephen's. Upper school students are required to complete a credit of Religious studies each year.

Location and Facilities
St. Stephen's campus is located in Houston's Museum District. Modeled after St. Thomas University's original campus, the school's buildings are a collection of 1930s-era homes that have been remodeled. All classrooms are designed to the specific requirements of a traditional Montessori classroom. Lower School classrooms are grouped not by grades but by multi-age groups, such as ages 3 to 6 years in a single classroom. Multi-age groups are an indication of an authentic Montessori educational facility.

Admissions
St. Stephen's features rolling enrollment, with application deadlines for early childhood students by December 31st. Applications may be sent one year in advance for enrollment. Before students are mailed the appropriate application material, parents must register a visitation appointment through the admission's office. St. Stephen's requires students entering 5th grade to 12th grade to take the ISEE. Students must obtain three teacher recommendation forms from their current English and math teacher as well as a teacher of their choice. Students must also submit a recommendation form from their current head of school, principal, or counselor.

Academic Tracks and Curriculum
The Montessori Method emphasizes the natural development of the student with the teacher acting as a guide and not as an instructor. Each classroom is open and orderly and is filled with Montessori materials, such as the pink tower of blocks. Students are allowed develop at their own pace, but within the specific limits of the classroom environment. From ages 2 ½ to 12 years, students participate in mixed age classrooms, where older students support younger students. St. Stephen's utilizes the traditional grading system of American education, assigning letter grades or numbers to exams. St. Stephen's incorporates the American system into the Montessori Method for grades 7 through 12.

Students must complete 25 credits and 90 hours of community service to graduate; one credit equals one year of study: English (4), History (4), Math (3), Science (3), Foreign Language (3), Religion (2), Wellness/Athletics (2), Technology & Senior Project (1), and Electives (3).

Special Needs
No information provided.

Foreign Languages
Students attending St. Stephen's must complete 3 years of a foreign language as a requirement for graduation. Students may choose to learn Spanish or French.

Arts
The pursuit of the fine arts is incorporated in the Montessori curriculum. Students are introduced to art using various materials in the Lower School. Students in the Upper School are given the option to take two years of Art as an elective. One course focuses on 2D design through painting and drawing. The second course focuses on 3D design using materials, such as clay, to create sculptures. Students may also participate in drama, which includes critiques on previously experienced theatre productions and researching the history of artistic eras.

Technology
St. Stephen's utilizes technology in every level of the school. Students in grades 7 through 12 are required to bring their laptops to school every day. St. Stephen's suggests that students bring a laptop that is no older than two years. Any Mac, PC, or Linux system with a wireless connection is acceptable. It is necessary for students to have Microsoft Office 2007 or newer installed on their laptop. Students in grades 7 through 12 are also assigned an email account through Microsoft Outlook Express and have access to classroom information and school events through Edline.

Extracurricular Activities
As part of the school's requirements for graduation, students must participate in community service starting in 7th grade. Students in 7th grade must complete 5 hours of community service, with each following grade completing an additional 5 hours from the year before; seniors will be expected to complete 30 hours of community service before they graduate. BOSS (Boys of St. Stephen's) and GLO (Girls Leadership Organization) determine the community service options for students, such as mentoring at the YMCA. Students also have the opportunity to participate in trips, such as traveling to Puerto Rico, Washington D.C., Mo Ranch, and the Grand Canyon.

Athletics
St. Stephen's includes physical activity within its curriculum and gives its students the chance to participate in various sports programs. Included in these sports programs are flag football, volleyball, golf, tennis, basketball, and soccer. St. Stephen's competes in the Texas Christian Athletics League and the Texas Association of Private and Parochial Schools league for both Middle School and High School students.

St. Stephen's Episcopal School Fast Facts

Overview

School Type	Montessori, Religious, Coeducational
Religious Affiliation	Episcopal
Date Founded	1971
Endowment	N/A
Grades Served	PreK-12th
Enrollment	170
Grade 12	13
Grade 11	9
Grade 10	12
Grade 9	14
Grade 8	10
Grade 7	11
Grade 6	6
Grade 5	5
Grade 4	8
Grade 3	7
Grade 2	4
Grade 1	7
Kindergarten	8
Pre-Kindergarten	56
Student to Teacher Ratio	6:1
Faculty with Advanced Degrees (# / %)	N/A
Minorities in Student Body	21%

Curriculum

Academic Tracks Offered	Montessori
Advanced Placement Courses Offered	N/A
Languages Offered	Spanish, French
Calendar (Semester / Trimester / Other)	Semester
Interscholastic Sports Programs	5

Graduating Seniors

National Merit Semi-Finalists (# / %)	0
Average SAT Scores (Class of 2010)	N/A
Mathematics	N/A
Critical Reading	N/A
Writing	N/A
% Students Admitted to 4 Year University	N/A

Admissions

Prime Entry Points	PreK, K, 1, 7, 9
Pre-K	$9,820-$11,775
Age 3 to 6 years	$10,290-$12,420
Grades 1-3	$13,135
Grades 4-6	$13,915
Grades 7-8	$13,990
Grade 9	$15,385
Grades 10-12	$16,785
Facilities Fee	$250
Students on Financial Aid	18%

St. Thomas Episcopal School

4900 Jackwood, Houston, TX 77096
713-666-3111
www.STES.org

Mr. Michael F. Cusack, Headmaster
Ms. Carin Thorn, Director of Admissions

Overview

Saint Thomas Episcopal School was founded in 1955 as a pre-school and kindergarten. It graduated its first high school class in 1967. Today, it offers thirteen years of instruction from Kindergarten Bridge through 12th grade. The school is accredited by Southwestern Association of Episcopal Schools, Houston Association of Independent Schools, and TAPPS.

Religious Affiliation

Saint Thomas is an institution of the Episcopal Diocese of Texas. All students attend Chapel every day; High School students participate in Bible Studies once a week. However, the school notes that "Chapel also gives an opportunity for diversity" since non-Episcopalians are allowed to limit their active participation during religious activities. The school does not have a Religion department or equivalent that offers further studies in Theology.

Location and Facilities

The school's primary campus is located on the southwest corner of the 610 Inner Loop in Houston's Meyerland area. The school shares a modest campus with St. Thomas' Episcopal Church. The campus is easily accessed off of Beechnut, South Rice, and Braeswood Boulevard. Affluent single-family homes line its west and south sides. Shopping centers are on its north and east. Additional athletic fields are located about 3 miles away from the main campus at 4113 Willowbend.

Admissions

Saint Thomas lists the following general criteria as necessary for admissions to the Upper School a) satisfactory score on an entrance exam b) academic transcripts for the past two years c) two teacher references from one math and one English teacher d) satisfactory interview with the Headmaster. The standardized test for the Middle and Upper Schools is the ISEE. Middle School students submit only one teacher recommendation. Lower school applicants take abbreviated versions of the Stanford Achievement test. Kindergarteners are assessed by a 30-minute school test. The school does give priority to siblings of currently enrolled students and members of St. Thomas' Episcopal Church.

Academic Tracks and Curriculum

A "Kindergarten Bridge" program is offered for students turning five in September or October. The curriculum is designed to bridge the gap between pre-school and kindergarten by reinforcing key materials. Children applying for kindergarten must be five years old on or before September 1st of their matriculation year.

Honors classes begin in the Middle School with the availability of Accelerated Algebra I in eighth grade. In addition to honors classes, the school offers fifteen AP classes including calculus and statistics. The school requires 25 credits for graduation; one credit is equivalent to one year of study: English (4), Math (4), Science (4), History (4), Foreign Latin (3), PE/ Band/ Dance (2), Electives (4).

Special Needs

The school designates seniors, juniors, and outstanding sophomores in high school as tutors for other students. Parents are responsible for all other arrangements including meeting time, place, and wages. Younger students may benefit from the school's

Study Buddies program whereby high school students help younger students with their homework and organizational skills.

Foreign Languages

Foreign language instruction is offered beginning in first grade with French. Required French study continues until fourth grade when students may then choose between French or Spanish. Greek is offered beginning in eighth grade. Three years of high school Latin study is required to graduate from Saint Thomas, and instruction is compulsory beginning in 6th grade. In addition to French, Latin, and Spanish, Upper School students may also study Chinese beginning in ninth grade. All languages are offered up to a fifth year level in high school with the exception of Chinese, offered through level IV.

Arts

The Fine Arts are treated as an elective at Saint Thomas's Upper School and include the performance and visual arts. All Upper School students may choose between Art, String Orchestra, Choir, and Theater Arts & Production. Additionally, seniors may take AP Studio Art. Band, Bagpipe Band, and Highland Dancing are part of the school's PE requirement. The school features a department of Scottish Arts.

Technology

Classroom based computer instruction begins in fourth grade when students begin learning to type and use Microsoft Office. In the Upper School, students may take Introduction and Principles of Computer Science.

Extracurricular Activities

Academic clubs include Junior Classical League, Mock Trial, Science Bowl, TAPPS Academic Team, and volunteering as a tutor for other students. Non-academic clubs include Chess Club, Cotillion, Scouting, and more. Students may participate in the Yearbook class beginning in ninth grade. Seniors and juniors may join the school's Upper School Honor Council and help educate and enforce the school's Honor Code.

Athletics

In the Middle School, students compete in the Greater Houston Athletic Conference (GHAC) in five sports: basketball, cross-country, softball, track & field, and volleyball. The Upper School fields sports teams across eight sports: basketball, cross-country, golf, soccer, swimming, tennis, track & field, and volleyball. Saint Thomas is a member of the Texas Association of Private and Parochial Schools (TAPPS).

St. Thomas Episcopal School Fast Facts

Overview
School Type	Religious, Coeducational
Religious Affiliation	Episcopal
Date Founded	1955
Endowment	N/A
Grades Served	KBr-12
Enrollment	648
Grade 12	44
Grade 11	48
Grade 10	48
Grade 9	51
Grade 8	56
Grade 7	50
Grade 6	53
Grade 5	49
Grade 4	43
Grade 3	51
Grade 2	50
Grade 1	47
Kindergarten	58
Student to Teacher Ratio	9:1
Faculty with Advanced Degrees (# / %)	N/A
Minorities in Student Body	35%

Curriculum
Academic Tracks Offered	On-Track, Honors, AP
Advanced Placement Courses Offered	15
Languages Offered	Chinese, French, Latin, Spanish
Calendar (Semester / Trimester / Other)	Semester
Interscholastic Sports Programs	8

Graduating Seniors
National Merit Semi-Finalists (# / %) 2011	2/5%
Average SAT Scores (Class of 2010)	1856
Mathematics	N/A
Critical Reading	N/A
Writing	N/A
% Students Admitted to 4 Year University	100%

Admissions
Prime Entry Points	K, 1, 6, 9
KBr – Grade 3	$11,351
Grades 4-5	$11,629
Grade 6	$12,743
Grades 7-8	$13,305
Grades 9-12	$14,277
Student Fee (KBr-5 / 6-12)	$325-$350
Facilities Fee	$325
Book Fee	$85-$160
Students on Financial Aid	N/A

St. Thomas High School

4500 Memorial Drive, Houston, TX 77007
713-864-6348
www.STHS.org

Rev. Ronald Schwenzer, President
Mr. Jon Moody, Director of Admissions

Overview

Three priests from the Congregation of St. Basil founded the school, then named St. Thomas College, in 1900 in an unused building of the Franciscan Monastery in downtown Houston. That first location in a warehouse was temporary as the school quickly moved to a location on Main Street in 1903. It moved to its current location in 1940.

Religious Affiliation

St. Thomas was founded by and remains an institution of the Basilian Fathers. The Basilian fathers are a Catholic religious congregation originating in France during the French Revolution. The Basilians became active in Texas beginning in the 1930's; the University of St. Thomas is also a Basilian institution. Approximately 20% of St. Thomas students are non-Catholic, but all students must participate in the school's religious activities.

Location and Facilities

The school's campus is centrally located within the 610 loop at the intersection of Shepherd and Memorial Drives. Buffalo Bayou is directly to its south. The DePelchin Children's Center is across Shepherd on the west side and the High School for Law Enforcement and Criminal Justice on the north side. An increasingly gentrifying community of young professionals lives to the East in apartments, town homes, and older single-family homes. The school's athletic facilities include two tennis courts, a multipurpose soccer/ football/ track stadium, baseball diamond, and multipurpose field. The campus also boasts a large, outdoor amphitheater.

Admissions

St. Thomas seeks to admit a socio-economically diverse group of students of average to well above average academic achievement. The school uses the following criteria when evaluating applicants: compatibility with the school, applicant's desire to attend school, HSPT scores, junior high school record, recommendations, and quality of application essay, and involvement in school activities. All applicants are personally interviewed upon the receipt of their completed application. The school does accept non-Catholic students, but everyone is required to take Theology classes, attend class retreats, and worship with the St. Thomas community.

Academic Tracks and Curriculum

St. Thomas offers three tracks—on track, honors, and Advanced Placement. Honors classes are offered beginning freshman year. Approximately 60% of students participate in at least one honors or AP class. Theology is required every year.

28 credits are required for graduation; each credit is equivalent to one year or two semesters—Theology (4), Mathematics (4), Social Studies (4), English (4), Science (4), Foreign Language (2), Technology (1), Health/ PE (2), Speech (.5), Fine Arts (.5), Electives (2).

Special Needs

No information provided.

Foreign Languages
Students are required to take two years of a language to meet graduation requirements. The school offers instruction in French, Latin, and Spanish up to four levels. AP Spanish is also offered.

Arts
St. Thomas requires one semester of a fine art to graduate. Students can choose from approximately 20 classes across the visual art, music, and theatre departments. Arts choices include photography, orchestra, jazz band, and theatre. Students host their own theatrical productions in the school's new Moran Fine Arts Center or join forces with the sister schools of Duchesne, Incarnate Word Academy, and St. Agnes.

Technology
Students are required to take two semesters of technology courses. Sophomores are required to take a course in computer applications where they learn about Microsoft Office and other applications. Juniors can choose between MS Office (intermediate/advanced), Visual Basic, and Java. Web design and advanced Java programming are offered as electives.

Extracurricular Activities
Clubs and organizations at St. Thomas include campus ministry, foreign language, art, music, speech and debate, student government, and student publications. The school publishes a list and descriptions of some clubs on its website. Approximately 95% of the student body participates in at least one extracurricular activity. The students publish an annual yearbook, annual literary magazine, and a biweekly or monthly newspaper.

Athletics
Students are required to complete four semesters of health/ physical education classes to graduate. All students are encouraged to try out for any of the school's interscholastic or intramural athletic teams. The school fields freshman, junior varsity, and varsity level teams in thirteen sports: baseball, basketball, cross-country, football, golf, lacrosse, roller hockey, rugby, soccer, swimming, track, tennis, wrestling. St. Thomas is a member of the Texas Association of Private and Parochial Schools (TAPPS).

St. Thomas High School Fast Facts

Overview

School Type	Religious, Boys
Religious Affiliation	Catholic
Date Founded	1900
Endowment	N/A
Grades Served	9-12
Enrollment	709
Grade 12	170
Grade 11	165
Grade 10	192
Grade 9	182
Student to Teacher Ratio	12:1
Faculty with Advanced Degrees	N/A
Minorities in Student Body	35%

Curriculum

Academic Tracks Offered	On-Track, Honors, AP
Advanced Placement Courses Offered	10
Languages Offered	French, Latin, Spanish
Calendar (Semester / Trimester / Other)	Semester
Interscholastic Sports Programs	13

Graduating Seniors

National Merit Semi-Finalists 2011 (# / %)	2 / 1%
Average SAT Scores (Class of 2011)	N/A
Mathematics	N/A
Critical Reading	N/A
Writing	N/A
% Students Admitted to 4 Year University	99%

Admissions

Prime Entry Points	9, 10
Grades 9-12	$13,250
Registration Fee	$400
Books	$250-$750
Students on Financial Aid	30%

Strake Jesuit College Preparatory

8900 Bellaire Boulevard, Houston, TX 77036   Fr. Daniel K. Lahart, President
713-774-7651   Mr. Scott Granito, Director of Admissions
www.StrakeJesuit.org

Overview

Father Michel F. Kennelly of the Jesuit Fathers of New Orleans Province founded Strake Jesuit in 1960 on land donated by the Strake family in what is now the Greater Sharpstown area. The school's first class of freshman matriculated in 1961. Although it remains at its original location, the school has grown tremendously since that time especially in the 1970s and in the 2000's. In the most recent decade, Strake undertook the *Greater Glory* Capital Campaign to vastly expand its facilities.

Religious Affiliation

Strake Jesuit is an institution sponsored by the Society of Jesus, a Catholic order of Priests and Brothers founded in 1540 by St. Ignatius of Loyola. Strake Jesuit is part of 50 Jesuit high schools in the United States.

Deeply rooted in the Roman Catholic Church tradition of teaching virtue and excellence, the Society of Jesus—following the example of its founder and influenced by the graces of the Spiritual Exercises—began its ministry to lay students in 1548, at the request of the citizens of Messina, Italy, where the Jesuits opened their first school. This Catholic and Jesuit tradition is at the heart of the school and influences the curriculum to daily rituals and even the teaching methodologies.

Students are not required to be Catholic but they must still take Theology every year and participate in the school's religious services. Strake Jesuit's religious education curriculum works to complement spiritual formation by developing the knowledge, attitudes, and behavior of Christian faith, values, and service among its students. At the very core of these formation programs is the Ignatian exercise of *cura personalis* (Latin meaning "care of the whole person").

Location and Facilities

Strake Jesuit's 44-acre campus is located in the Greater Sharptstown area of southwest Houston. It is fairly equidistant between the Sam Houston Tollway, Westpark Tollway, and Highway 59. Its campus is adjacent to St. Agnes Academy off of Bellaire Boulevard. The school's adjacent location to St. Agnes allows the two schools to share some course offerings.

The campus is often described as college like in that it is comprised of many non-connected structures built over the years. The School's *Greater Glory* Capital Campaign was responsible for many new structures completed by 2009 including the three-story Clay Activity Center, Lahart Chapel of St. Ignatius, Moran Dining Hall, and expansive athletic facilities. Strake's new athletic complex includes a 3,000-seat competition gym, separate gym housing three basketball courts, Capt. Andrew Houghton Weight Room, heated, 8-lane competition pool, and four lighted tennis courts. The baseball field opened in 2003, and the 5,000-seat multi-purpose stadium opened in 2004.

Admissions

Strake Jesuit advises that applicants should be a) academically prepared to handle the school's curriculum b) willing to study consistently and diligently outside of class c) be receptive to the school's Catholic heritage and traditions. Strake's application requires recommendations from a math teacher, English teacher, and a principal or counselor. The school requires that applicants sit for the HSPT, usually administered at the school in January.

Academic Tracks and Curriculum
Strake Jesuit offers a college preparatory curriculum. It also offers Accelerated and Advanced Placement courses. Strake Jesuit offers 10 accelerated and 12 AP courses. Freshmen are not allowed to take accelerated or AP classes; typically all students are limited to three accelerated or AP classes at any given time. The school offers some non-traditional courses in social studies such as business law, business and personal finance, and African American Studies. Likewise, the school's Theology department offers fifteen classes. All students must take a theology course each year. Some classes are offered by St. Agnes, the sister school directly adjacent to Strake Jesuit. Seniors must have accumulated 100 hours of community service in order to graduate.

Strake requires students to complete 27.5 credits to graduate; one credit is equivalent to one year of study: English (4), Mathematics (4), Science (4), Social Studies (4), Language (3), Computer Science (1), Theology (4), PE/ Health (2), Communication & Fine Arts (1), Community Service of 100 hours (.5).

Special Needs
No information provided.

Foreign Languages
Three years of foreign language instruction are required for a diploma at Strake Jesuit. Students can choose between Chinese, French, Latin, or Spanish. Spanish and Latin are offered up to the AP level, French up to an honors fourth year—the school combines years 4 and 5 into one class. Chinese is a new offering at the school beginning in the 2011-2012 academic year.

Arts
Strake Jesuit combines communication classes and fine arts into the same department. Students are required to take at least one class from this department to graduate. There are more than thirty-classes from which to choose, including several classes in TV broadcasting and production.

Technology
The school has two computer laboratories with more than sixty computers. Internet access is via the school's dedicated, super high-speed T-1 line. All students have their own password protected user accounts and allocated hard drive space. Students are not required to have laptops at school. At least one credit of computer science is required to graduate. Students choose from 5 classes including AP Computer Science.

Extracurricular Activities
Students can participate in more than fifty clubs. The clubs on campus are extensive, including diversity organizations like the Black and Hispanic Student Unions and sports organizations like Intramural Sports. The Student Council is composed of eleven elected representatives from each grade and four officers from the senior class.

Athletics
All students must take 1.5 credit hours (or three semester classes) of physical education and .5 credit hours (one semester) of health. The school offers "athletic PE" classes whereby students involved in a sport can further hone their skills in that sport and satisfy the PE requirement; however, approval of the sport's head coach is required to participate. The school participates in thirteen interscholastic sports: baseball, basketball, cross-country, football, golf, lacrosse, rugby, soccer, swimming, tennis, track, water polo, and wrestling. Students can participate in a sport at the freshman, junior varsity, and varsity levels. Strake Jesuit is a member of the University Interscholastic League (UIL).

Strake Jesuit Fast Facts

Overview

School Type	Religious, Boys
Religious Affiliation	Catholic
Date Founded	1960
Endowment	N/A
Grades Served	9-12
Enrollment	902
Grade 12	218
Grade 11	213
Grade 10	224
Grade 9	247
Student to Teacher Ratio	15:1
Faculty with Advanced Degrees (# / %)	N/A
Minorities in Student Body	39%

Curriculum

Academic Tracks Offered	On-Track, Honors, AP
Advanced Placement Courses Offered	12
Languages Offered	Chinese, French, Latin, Spanish
Calendar (Semester / Trimester / Other)	Semester
Interscholastic Sports Programs	13

Graduating Seniors

National Merit Semi-Finalists (# / %)	10/5%
Average SAT Scores (Class of 2011)	1887
Mathematics	642
Critical Reading	619
Writing	626
% Students Admitted to 4 Year University	99%

Admissions

Prime Entry Points	9
Grades 9-12	$15,150
Books and Supplies	$500
Students on Financial Aid	13%

T.H. Rogers Middle School

5840 San Felipe St., Houston, TX 77057
713-917-3565
www.ms.houstonisd.org/THRogers

Mr. Dave Muzyka, Principal
Ms. Leslie Gonsalves, Magnet Coordinator

Overview

Founded in 1962, T.H. Rogers sees itself as "a lighthouse beacon that safely guides all children into harbors of success." T.H. Rogers School consists of three sub-schools: MI-PSI, Program for the Deaf and Hard of Hearing (PDHH), and the Vanguard Program. MI-PSI serves students who have severe disabilities in cognitive and developmental areas. The PDHH encourages teachers to help their students learn by using a variety of communication techniques, such as speech, listening, lip reading, Conceptually Accurate Signed English (CASE), ASL, and Visual Phonics. The Vanguard Program caters to Gifted and Talented (G/T) students through academics, creativity, and leadership.

Religious Affiliation

As a public school, T.H. Rogers has no religious affiliation. According to Houston Independent School District's policy, every school has a moment of silence each day during which students can pray silently to themselves if they so choose. Also, absences because of religious holidays do not count toward the student's total number of absences. However, the student is still responsible for the makeup work.

Location and Facilities

Located at the corner of San Felipe St. and Bering Drive, T.H. Rogers resides in the Greater Uptown area, a little northwest of the Galleria. The school resides next to St. George Place Elementary, Trotter Family YMCA, and Westminster United Methodist Church. T.H. Rogers's facilities include four baseball fields, four campus buildings, and a playground.

Admissions

For the Vanguard Program, in addition to an application, T.H. Rogers requires testing, which is offered on two Saturdays in January for students starting in grades 1-8. In order to see if a student qualifies for the Vanguard program, the admissions coordinator uses test scores, report card grades, teacher observation, and parent rating. At T.H. Rogers, kindergarten and 6th grade are the entry-level grades, and T.H. Rogers reserves twenty-five percent of the available spaces for siblings of former and current students. Since T.H. Rogers has a limited number of spaces available, the qualified candidates are put into a lottery if there are more applicants than spaces.

Academic Tracks and Curriculum

In the Vanguard Program, the curriculum is advanced (Pre-AP) and interdisciplinary for all students. In addition to core courses, T.H. Rogers offers the following electives: art, choral music, orchestra, broadcast media, conversational sign language, reading/math lab, robotics, research, numerous technology classes, drama, journalism, and yearbook.

Special Needs

Standard HISD policies.

Foreign Languages

In its foreign language program, T.H. Rogers offers Chinese, Spanish, and French.

Arts
The Vanguard Program offers classes in orchestra, choral music, scholastic art and writing, Texas art, and musings. It also has music appreciation, drama, journalism, and yearbook classes.

Technology
No information provided.

Extracurricular Activities
Vanguard offers the following clubs and academic competition opportunities: chess, Scholastic Writing, Math Counts, National French Contest, National Spanish Exam, Name That Book, Geography Bee, History Fair, Science Fair, Scholastic Art, Choral Music, Spelling Bee, UIL Orchestra, Prep Bowl, Ecobot Challenge, and First Lego League Challenge. The school also hosts the following student leadership opportunities: Student Council, National Junior Honor Society, and Peer Mediation. At Vanguard, students participate in the following service projects: Camp MI-Way, Community Volunteering, Sixth Grade Service Unit, and School-Wide Global Project

Athletics
T.H. Rogers offers a number of after-school sports throughout the year. The boys' sports include: baseball, basketball, cross-country, soccer, swimming, and track. The girls' sports include: volleyball, basketball, cross- country, soccer, swimming, and track.

T.H. Rogers Middle School Fast Facts

Overview

School Type	Public, Magnet, Coeducational
Religious Affiliation	None
Date Founded	1962
Grades Served	6th-8th
Enrollment	396
Grade 8	122
Grade 7	138
Grade 6	136
Student to Teacher Ratio	10:1
Faculty with Advanced Degrees (# / %)	17/37%
Minorities in Student Body	74%

Curriculum

Academic Tracks Offered	Pre-AP
International Baccalaureate Courses	N/A
Languages Offered	French, Spanish, Chinese
Calendar (Semester / Trimester / Other)	Semester
Interscholastic Sports Programs	7

Public School Stats

Gifted and Talented Students	79%
Free & Reduced Lunch	34%
AYP (2006-2011)	Met AYP
TEA Accountability (2006-2007)	Recognized
TEA Accountability (2007-2010)	Exemplary
TEA Accountability (2010-2013)	Recognized

The Village School

13077 Westella Drive, Houston, TX 77077
281-496-7900
www.TheVillageSchool.com

Ms. Monica Garza, Head of School
Mr. Erik Srnka, Director of Admissions

Overview

The Village School began as an early childhood education facility in 1966, expanding to include Pre-Kindergarten to 4th grade students by 1983. During the ten years that followed, The Village School moved to its current location in West Houston and introduced 5th, 6th, 7th, and 8th grades to its curriculum. In 2006, the school joined the Meritas Family of Schools, a for-profit company of ten college preparatory schools found across the globe. Dr. Jonathan Silver, the then Head of School, introduced the high school program in 2008, with the first 12th grade class beginning in the fall of 2011.

Religious Affiliation

The Village School does not have any religious affiliation.

Location and Facilities

The Village School is located in Houston's "energy corridor," between Memorial Drive and Westheimer, just west of Dairy Ashford. The campus rests on 18 acres of land, with a 70,000 square foot facility for Pre-K through 8th grade and a 50,000 square foot facility for the high school program. 8 of the 18 acres are reserved for future developments, but currently hold a 30,000 square foot facility.

Admissions

The Village School features a rolling admissions policy. Pre-Kindergarten and Kindergarten applicants must participate in a Group Visit and take the WPPSI Assessment. 1st grade applicants must also participate in a Group Visit and take the WISC. Students applying to the 2nd to 4th grade must take the Stanford Achievement Test and the OLSAT, while students applying to 5th through 12th grade must complete the ISEE and OLSAT. The Village School requires all applicants to complete the tests with an accredited testing agent at The Village School, although permission may be given to complete a test at an approved facility outside of The Village School. Applicants must submit Teacher Recommendation Forms along with their application:

- Pre-K and Kindergarten: 1 shared teacher recommendation
- Grades 1 to 5: 1 teacher recommendation
- Grades 6 to 12: 1 English teacher and 1 math teacher recommendation

All students are required to submit transcripts and school records to The Village School. 6th to 12th grade applicants will participate in a Student Interview that will be scheduled by The Village School's faculty after reviewing the student's application.

Academic Tracks and Curriculum

The Village School develops a Personal Learning Plan for each student, which is a goal-oriented process that requires the student to become more responsible for his/her own education. Teachers utilize differentiation in the classroom, a method of instruction, which puts students into small groups to work on specific activities. The Village School offers the International Baccalaureate Programme to its 11th and 12th grade students. However, students in 9th and 10th grade follow a curriculum that is designed to be similar to the IB Programme. Before their junior year, students must choose one of five Honors Houses:

- Math, Science & Technology (MST)
- Comparative Languages & Literature (CLL)

- Markets, Entrepreneurs & Globalization (MEG)
- Arts – Studio or Performing (ASP)
- International Studies (SB)

Once chosen, students must complete their chosen Honors House's courses, Humanities I & II, two credits in Athletics and the arts, English 11 & 12, and electives. For the sciences, The Village School has modified the traditional order and has its 9th graders begin with physics, its 10th graders complete chemistry, and its 11th and 12th graders choose from advanced courses in biology, chemistry, and physics.

Special Needs
No information provided.

Foreign Languages
The Village School offers Latin, French, and Spanish.

Arts
Students attending The Village School have the opportunity to participate in a number of fine arts programs. For the musical arts, students may join Band, Choir, Orchestra and Jazz Band and may participate in the Meritas European Band Tour, Meritas International Theater Festival, and the Meritas Music Festival. For the visual arts, students may take courses such as Sculpture, Digital Photography, and Ceramics. For the theater arts, students may join the STARS Performance Group, which consists of a troupe for the lower and middle schools and a troupe for the high school. The Village School hosts a dance program for Pre-K through the 12th grade, with opportunities to participate in the Meritas European Charity Tour and the Meritas Dance Festival.

Technology
The Village School hosts three computer labs and SMART Boards in each classroom. The school also features the Touchpoints program, which connects all Meritas schools via videoconference for debates on a variety of subjects between their students.

Extracurricular Activities
Students of all ages have access to a number of clubs and organizations at The Village School, including several fine arts and athletics programs. Lower School students may join the Chess Club, Destination Imagination program, and the Private Schools Interscholastic Association (provides various competitions between students of different private schools). Middle School students may join the Math and Science Team, Speech and Debate Team, Student Council, Pep Club, and the National Junior Honor Society. High School students may join a larger assortment of clubs than their younger classmates, such as Viking Way (high school students interact with Lower School students) or Be the Change Leadership, a community service club.

Athletics
As early as 6th grade, students have the opportunity to participate in The Village School's athletics program. Boys may participate in Cross Country, Football, Basketball, Soccer, Baseball, Lacrosse, Tennis, Golf, and Track & Field. Girls may participate in Cross Country, Volleyball, Basketball, Cheerleading, Soccer, Softball, Tennis, Track & Field, Golf, and Lacrosse.

The Village School Fast Facts

Overview

School Type	Independent, Coeducational
Religious Affiliation	Nonsectarian
Date Founded	1966
Endowment	N/A
Grades Served	PreK-12th
Enrollment	788
Grade 12	New
Grade 11	New
Grade 10	51
Grade 9	50
Grade 8	74
Grade 7	11
Grade 6	77
Grade 5	77
Grade 4	80
Grade 3	66
Grade 2	64
Grade 1	79
Kindergarten	85
Pre-Kindergarten	74
Student to Teacher Ratio	9:1
Faculty with Advanced Degrees (#/%)	N/A
Minorities in Student Body	55%

Curriculum

Academic Tracks Offered	On Track, IB
International Baccalaureate Classes	N/A
Languages Offered	Latin, Spanish, French
Calendar (Semester / Trimester / Other)	Semester
Interscholastic Sports Programs	11

Graduating Seniors

National Merit Semi-Finalists (#/%)	2/4%
Average SAT Scores (Class of 2010)	N/A
Mathematics	N/A
Critical Reading	N/A
Writing	N/A
% Students Admitted to 4 Year University	N/A

Admissions

Prime Entry Points	PreK, K, 1, 6, 9
Pre-School	$10,975
Pre-K and Kindergarten	$16,375
Grades 1-2	$17,875
Grade 3	$17,975
Grade 4	$18,060
Grade 5	$18,300
Grades 6-7	$20,400
Grade 8	$21,300
Grades 9-11	$20,925
Grade 12	$21,275
Students on Financial Aid	N/A

Westchester Academy for International Studies

901 Yorkchester, Houston, TX 77079
713-251-1800
WAIS.SpringBranchISD.com

Dr. Natalie Blasingame, Director
Ms. Andrea Andrews, Registrar

Overview

Westchester Academy for International Studies, a charter school, originally opened in 1967 as Westchester High School to accommodate a surge in enrollment for Memorial High School. Westchester opened with eighteen hundred students and grew to four thousand in seven years, prompting the opening of Stratford High School near Westchester. In 1985, Westchester High School was closed and its students transferred to Stratford and Memorial due to a decrease in enrollment. After the completion of a large renovation project, the school reopened in 2001 as Westchester Academy for International Studies. Westchester now supports sixth through twelfth grade students and provides the International Baccalaureate Diploma for its high school students. Westchester is currently developing a certified Middle Years IB Program.

Religious Affiliation

As a public school, Westchester has no religious affiliation. According to Spring Branch Independent School District's policy, every school has a moment of silence each day during which students can pray silently to themselves if they so choose. Also, absences because of religious holidays do not count toward the student's total number of absences. However, the student is still responsible for the makeup work.

Location and Facilities

Located at the corner of Yorkchester Drive and Patchester Drive, Westchester's 8-acre lot contains its main campus, multiple support buildings, and two parking lots. Westchester's athletic facilities include a baseball field, football field (surrounded by a track), two soccer fields, four tennis courts, and a gym.

Admissions

Students and parents must complete and submit an application, which includes Assurances and a Family-School Commitment Form, along with the student's most recent report card and transcript (applicants for tenth to twelfth grade) to Westchester Academy. The student must also be a resident of Spring Branch ISD and demonstrate proof to that fact. Some applicants will be asked to participate in an interview with some of Westchester's faculty. Eligible applicants are then enrolled on a space available basis. If there are more applicants than available spaces, then the eligible applicants will be entered into a lottery. Siblings of current Westchester students will be offered enrollment before the lottery takes place. In the event there are more Eligible Siblings than available spaces, a lottery will take place.

Academic Tracks and Curriculum

Westchester only provides an advanced curriculum via IB and AP courses. Students are expected to take part in the IB program in full or by taking specific subjects as part of the program. As the IB program continues to develop, the school will offer more IB courses in place of AP courses. Students may also earn college credit through SBISD's Early College program by taking courses at Houston Community College.

In order to graduate with a Recommended Diploma, students must complete 26 credits; one credit is equivalent to one year of study: English (4), Social Studies (4), Math (4), Science (4), Foreign Language (2), Physical Education (1), Speech (1/2), Fine Art (1), and Electives (5 and 1/2). A Distinguished Diploma requires one more year of a foreign language.

In order to graduate with an International Baccalaureate Diploma, students are required to complete six subjects, three "Higher Level" and three "Standard Level" courses. These subjects include: first language, second language, math, science, social science, and an IB elective. Students must also complete 150 hours of CAS (community, action, and service), a 4,000-word research essay, and a capstone course titled "Theory of Knowledge."

Special Needs
As a charter school, Westchester is not as bound by state laws as a public school. While Westchester will admit students with learning differences, students are expected to meet the school's curriculum requirements. The ARD committee and Westchester faculty will be the deciding body as to whether or not a position at Westchester is appropriate for the applicant with learning differences. Students who do not and cannot meet the expectations of the school will be asked to return to their home school.

Foreign Languages
Westchester offers students a number of foreign languages, which is required by the IB Program. Students may take AP and IB courses in Spanish Literature and Language, German, and French. Students may also take an IB course in Italian. Students attending Westchester from Cedar Brook Elementary will continue SBISD's Dual Language Secondary Program. If an applicant to seventh or eighth grade has not previously earned a credit in a foreign language, then the student will not be allowed to take a foreign language course until the student's ninth grade year, unless they are a native speaker and test accordingly.

Arts
Westchester students may take IB courses in Music, Theater Arts, and Visual Arts. Students may also participate in Choir.

Technology
Westchester provides several technology courses: Web Mastery, Robotics, Design Cycle, Computers, Animation, Programming, and Multimedia.

Extracurricular Activities
Westchester hosts a number of clubs and organizations for its students: dance, Model United Nations, Chess, comedy, aquatics, knitting, National Honors Society, student council, and service organizations. Students are expected to participate in at least one club while attending Westchester.

Athletics
Westchester does not support any UIL sports, but the school does host a number of sports clubs. Students may participate in the Spartan Lacrosse Club (boys), Meatheads Weightlifting Club, Middle School Soccer Club, and the Tennis Club. Westchester students may participate in the UIL sports programs at their home (zoned) schools.

Westchester Academy for International Studies Fast Facts

Overview
School Type	Public, Charter, Coeducational
Religious Affiliation	None
Date Founded	1967
Endowment	N/A
Grades Served	6 – 12
Enrollment	977
Grade 12	143
Grade 11	145
Grade 10	149
Grade 9	154
Grade 8	135
Grade 7	134
Grade 6	142
Student to Teacher Ratio	13:1
Faculty with Advanced Degrees	83/50%
Minorities in Student Body	64%

Curriculum
Academic Tracks Offered	IB, AP, Pre-AP
Advanced Placement Courses Offered	14
Languages Offered	Spanish, German, French, Italian
Calendar (Semester / Trimester / Other)	Semester
Interscholastic Sports Programs	0

Graduating Seniors
National Merit Semi-Finalists 2011 (# / %)	0/0%
Average SAT Scores (Class of 2011)	1581
Mathematics	526
Critical Reading	536
Writing	519
% Students Admitted to 4 Year University	80%

Public School Stats
Gifted and Talented Students	14%
Free & Reduced Lunch	51%
AYP (2012)	Met AYP
TEA Accountability (2010-2011)	Exemplary

This is one of those intentionally left blank pages. If it weren't blank, the next page would be on the wrong side of a double-sided page!

Appendix

Data Sources and Profile Criteria

In crafting our survey of Houston's private schools, we kept certain criteria in mind. We wanted to know the breadth and scope of the each school's curriculum and academic tracks. We wanted to know what sports programs, fine arts programs, technology programs, and extracurricular activities are hosted at each school. We wanted to know the requirements for admission and whether or not a school has a religious affiliation.

Sources of Information

Compiling the information you see here was an arduous and time-consuming task that involved multiple resources:

- School websites and publications
- School Administrators
- Parents, Students, and Tutors – we asked our own client parents and students who attend these schools to help us fill in the gaps; also some of our employed tutors are alumni from the schools we profiled, and they provided additional insight
- National Center for Education Statistics – most recent information is from the 2009-2010 school year; most of our information about number of number of students, racial makeup, and student to teacher ratio come from this survey
- National Merit Scholarship Corporation – the Non-profit publishes a list of National Merit Semi-Finalists each year by school
- OpenEndowment.org, Guidestar.org, and publicly available financial statements – when available, we used these sources to discern the endowments of schools
- "An Introduction to School Finance in Texas." TTARA Research Foundation. January 2012 – This publication was useful in clarifying how Texas finances public education.

School Profile Information

History

- When was the school founded?
- Is the school at its original location?
- What is the background of the school's founders?
- What background information on the school represents the objectives of the school?

Religious Affiliation

- Does the school have a religious affiliation?
- What is the history of that affiliation?
- If the school is nonsectarian, what is the school's policy towards religion?
- Does the school accept students of various faiths?
- How is religion incorporated into the school's curriculum?

Location and Facilities

- What is the physical location of the school's campus?
- What academic and athletic facilities are available on school grounds?
- When were the facilities built?
- Are there future construction plans?
- What type of neighborhood surrounds the school?

Admissions

- Does the school offer an online application or only a physical copy?
- What are the requirements for the application process?
  - ISEE vs. HSPT
  - Photo
  - Teacher Recommendation Forms (Type)
  - Student's religious background
  - Testing requirements
- Are there any special requirements for admission in comparison to other private schools?
- Is "shadowing" required?
- Is an interview required?
- What kind of student does the school look for?
- Is legacy a factor in the admissions process?
- How selective is the school?

Academic Tracks and Curriculum

- What type of academic tracks does the school offer?
  - On Track (Regular Track)
  - Honors Track
  - Advanced Placement Track
  - Montessori
  - International Baccalaureate
- What are the school's graduation requirements?
- Are there any special courses offered in comparison to other private schools?
- How many AP courses are available?
- When can students start taking honors and AP classes?
- Is there a limit to how many advanced classes a student can take?

Special Needs

- Does the school have the capability and/or desire to work with special needs students?
- What type of accommodations does the school provide for students with learning disabilities?
- What types of programs are available to students, such as mentorship programs?

Foreign Languages

- What foreign languages are available at the school?

- What are the school's graduation requirements for foreign language credit?
- Does the school offer Advanced Placement Foreign Language courses?
- How is the school's foreign language program integrated into the school's curriculum?

Arts

- What fine arts programs are available at the school?
- How does the school integrate fine arts into its curriculum?
- What special events are available for fine arts exhibits and performances?

Technology

- What is the school's technology policy?
- Does the school allow students to use their laptops in the classroom?
- Does the school provide students with laptops/tablets?
- What technology is used in the classroom?
- What computers are used in the school's computer labs?

Extracurricular Activities

- What clubs are hosted by the school?
- What organizations are hosted by the school?
- What kind of community service opportunities does the school provide?

Athletics

- When are the school's sports programs available to its student body?
- What association does the school's sports programs compete in?
- What sports are offered only for boys?
- What sports are offered only for girls?
- What sports are offered for co-ed?

Corporate Profile

About General Academic

Since our incorporation in 2003, our superior insight and institutional capabilities and organization have assisted over 1000 students in Houston and around the world. Today, General Academic's operations include in-home tutoring and office based solutions. Our new office, the Study Lounge, in the Rice Village is a one-of-a-kind lively, coffeehouse-like environment to make students feel comfortable and excited about getting down to business.

Primary Service Offerings

One-To-One, In-Home and In-Office Tutoring
Our team of current Rice undergraduates, graduates, and recent Top Tier alumni provide subject tutoring in virtually all subjects and skill areas ranging from physics to Chinese to SAT prep. We develop a custom strategy and road map to ensure that your student obtains the success you seek.

Walk-In Homework Help + Skills Assessment in the Rice Village
The Study Lounge is a new concept that combines the feel of a cozy coffee house with the support of our brilliant tutor Analysts. No appointment is required; when your student needs help, just show up and sign-in. The tutor Analyst on duty will check-in your student and ensure that he or she works through an agenda. Access is by monthly, unlimited subscription or hourly fee.

SAT and ACT Prep Small Classes in the Rice Village
Our SAT and ACT curricula are a holistic and comprehensive solution designed to prepare your student for these college admissions tests in eight weeks or less. Our instructors scored in the top 1% of all test takers. Classes are limited to just 8 students and include unlimited extra help in our Study Lounge.

ISEE and HSPT Prep Small Classes in the Rice Village
Our ISEE and HSPT preparation classes will help ensure that middle school students will have the skills, strategies, and confidence they need to succeed on these private high school entrance exam tests. Classes are limited to just 8 students and include unlimited extra help in our Study Lounge.

Summer Courses: Get Inspired, Get Ahead
Our summer offerings include test and application preparation (SAT, ACT, ISEE, HSPT, College Apps) and enrichment courses. Enrichment courses regularly include Creative Writing, Computer Building, Chinese, Study Skills and more. Enrollment is limited to just eight students.

The Corporate Anti-Corporate Advantage

We strive to offer quality, personalized services at competitive rates. Our small size and local ownership enable us to more closely tailor our services to your individual needs. Simultaneously, our strong management and corporate identity ensure that you receive a high quality and well supported product.

Contact Information
1-800-750-2060 | 2339 University Blvd, Suite C, Houston, TX 77005 |
Mail@GeneralAcademic.com

CPSIA information can be obtained at www.ICGtesting.com
Printed in the USA
LVOW021648111212

311166LV00003B/71/P

9 781105 873188